Not Just Good, but Beautiful

EDITED BY STEVEN LOPES AND HELEN ALVARÉ

Not Just Good, but Beautiful

The Complementary Relationship Between Man and Woman

*Pope Francis, Rick Warren, Johann Christoph Arnold,
N. T. Wright, Jonathan Sacks, Jacqueline C. Rivers,
Tsui-Ying Sheng, Russell D. Moore, M. Prudence Allen,
Wael Farouq, Gerhard Müller, Kala Acharya,
Nissho Takeuchi, Henry B. Eyring,
Ignacio Ibarzábal, Jean Laffitte*

Plough Publishing House

Published by Plough Publishing House
Walden, New York
Robertsbridge, England
Elsmore, Australia
www.plough.com

Front cover image courtesy Humanum.
Photograph on page 1: AP Photo/Bullit Marquez

ISBN: 978-0-87486-683-4

20 19 18 17 16 15   1 2 3 4 5 6 7 8 9

A catalog record for this book is available from the British Library
Library of Congress Cataloging-in-Publication Data pending

Printed in the United States of America

Contents

Preface

From November 17 through 19, 2014, Rome bore witness to an extraordinary gathering of four hundred scholars and religious leaders from around the world, convening in an international colloquium to discuss the complementarity of man and woman in marriage. Opened by Pope Francis, sponsored by the Congregation for the Doctrine of the Faith, and co-hosted by the Pontifical Council for the Family, the Pontifical Council for Interreligious Dialogue, and the Pontifical Council for the Promotion of Christian Unity, the Humanum colloquium brought religious leaders into direct discussion with scholars, researchers, family counselors, social workers, and community organizers – all for the single purpose of reflecting together on the fundamental good of the complementary union of man and woman.

The mere existence of such a broad-based gathering, and the obvious goodwill among the participants, is already an affirmation that the joyful truth of the complementarity of man and woman in marriage is not a sectarian proposition or a belief limited to one or another religious group. Rather, the great religious traditions of the world together recognize that the truth of marriage is something written on the human heart by a loving Creator. Thus this initiative is born of the conviction that the union of husband and wife in marriage offers a vital contribution to the flourishing of spouses, children, communities, and whole societies.

The gathering was called Humanum: An International Colloquium on the Complementarity of Man and Woman. "Humanum" signifies man and woman together – humanity in the image of a loving God, the creator of all life and the origin of human society. As a term, "complementarity" is sometimes misused and misconstrued to imply the subjugation of one sex to the other. At its core, however, it encompasses the equality of women and men while neither obscuring nor diminishing their differences.

Complementarity entails a reciprocity wherein men and women depend upon each other and learn from each other; it benefits spouses directly while also being open, receptive, and life-giving. Perhaps at this historical moment, when so many other models of relationships are proposed and promoted without sufficient reflection, the common testimony of believers from various traditions on the creative power of man and woman together can be a source of hope and inspiration to people of goodwill everywhere.

The international, ecumenical, and interreligious character of Humanum is particularly helpful in removing the discussion of marriage from the realm of politics and setting it on a firmer and more enlightening foundation. In the colloquium presentations gathered in this volume, the authors draw upon their religious conviction, yes, but also upon philosophy, sociology, psychology, and the biological sciences in order to consider the bodily and spiritual nature of the human person and the intrinsic meaning of marriage. There is also substantial consideration of the needs of the poor, of young people, and of the challenges posed when more privileged nations attempt to impose ideological and political notions about the family onto other nations.

Indeed, the breadth of so many different perspectives on complementarity, taken together, offers eloquent witness to the interrelatedness of man and woman, male and female. At the same time, the different authors highlight varying aspects of the ways the sexes relate in a complementary manner. Some emphasize how each sex takes on some of the other's gifts and then expresses them in a way particular to the sex of the recipient. Others highlight the unique way that one sex can draw out the best from the other, and supply the needs of the other in a marvellous synergy that certainly regards procreation and the raising of children, but also permeates every other interaction and activity of the spouses. Following upon these reflections, the colloquium participants affirm that political attempts to redefine the essence of marriage, while neglecting this source of nuptial dynamism, ignore something that is fundamental to the nature of human relationships. Such attempts cannot succeed.

Humanum does not overlook the concrete, pastoral implications of this conversation about marriage. Discussions within the Catholic Church during the recent Synod of Bishops have underscored the importance of new language to describe the nature and genius of marriage and family life, language that might propose the beauty of marriage to a world grown tired of a conversation that focuses only on problems in relationships, divorce, declining marriage rates, and the like. Relatively little energy has been devoted to a robust discussion about the creative power of the complementary union, or dynamic strategies to support marriage and families. The fourteen religious traditions represented by the Humanum speakers offer proposals drawn from the wisdom of those cultures and traditions about marriage and the intrinsic value of parenting and community formation. The texts collected in this volume offer a rich treasure of new language and insights into the family at its starting point: the husband and wife. They are intelligent and moving, beautiful and rational at one and the same time.

This collection of presentations is offered as a contribution to a discussion that must continue. By considering carefully what marriage involves at its core – the complementary relationship of man and woman – we contribute to the development of what Pope Francis calls a new human ecology, one which affirms equality in dignity and respects the diversity of women and men. The colloquium was indeed a unique occasion for discussion, cooperation, and common witness on a matter of fundamental human importance. But one such gathering can never be the final word. With this volume, I invite your participation in continuing the conversation of Humanum so that this new human ecology may flourish.

Gerhard Cardinal Müller
Prefect of the Congregation for the Doctrine of the Faith
The Vatican, March 30, 2015

"To reflect upon complementarity is nothing less than to ponder the dynamic harmonies at the heart of all Creation. . . . It is not just a good thing, but it is also beautiful."

POPE FRANCIS

I

POPE FRANCIS

Not Just Good, but Beautiful

I WOULD LIKE TO BEGIN by sharing with you a reflection on the title of your colloquium. "Complementarity" is a precious word, with multiple meanings. It can refer to situations where one of two things adds to, completes, or fulfills a lack in the other. But complementarity is much more than that. Christians find its deepest meaning in the First Letter to the Corinthians, where Saint Paul tells us that the Spirit has endowed each of us with different gifts so that – just as the human body's members work together for the good of the whole – everyone's gifts can work together for the benefit of each (1 Cor. 12). To reflect upon "complementarity" is nothing less than to ponder the dynamic harmonies at the heart of all creation. This is the key word, harmony. All complementarities were made by our Creator, because the Holy Spirit, who is the Author of harmony, achieves this harmony.

It is fitting that you have gathered here in this international colloquium to explore the complementarity of man and woman. This complementarity is at the root of marriage and family, which is the first school where we learn to appreciate our own and others' gifts, and where we begin to acquire the arts of living together. For most of us, the family provides the principal place where we can begin to "breathe" values and ideals, as well to realize our full capacity for virtue and charity. At the same time, as we know, families are places of tensions: between egoism and altruism, reason and passion, immediate desires and long-range goals. But families also provide frameworks for resolving such tensions. This is important. When we speak of complementarity between man and woman in this context, let us not confuse that term with the simplistic idea that all the roles and relations of the two sexes are fixed in a single, static pattern. Complementarity will take many forms as each man and woman brings his or her distinctive contributions to their marriage and to the formation of their children – his or her personal richness, personal charisma. Complementarity becomes a great wealth. It is not just a good thing but it is also beautiful.

In our day, marriage and the family are in crisis. We now live in a culture of the temporary, in which more and

---

✦ POPE FRANCIS *is the leader of the Catholic Church. Before he was elected to the papacy on March 13, 2013, he was Cardinal Jorge Mario Bergoglio of Argentina. He is the first Jesuit pope, the first from the Americas, and the first to take the name Francis, inspired by Saint Francis of Assisi, whom he has called "the man of the poor, the man of peace, the man who loved and cared for creation."*

more people are simply giving up on marriage as a public commitment. This revolution in manners and morals has often flown the flag of freedom, but in fact it has brought spiritual and material devastation to countless human beings, especially the poorest and most vulnerable. Evidence is mounting that the decline of the marriage culture is associated with increased poverty and a host of other social ills, disproportionately affecting women, children, and the elderly. It is always they who suffer the most in this crisis.

The crisis in the family has produced a crisis of human ecology, for social environments, like natural environments, need protection. And although the human race has come to understand the need to address conditions that menace our natural environments, we have been slower to recognize that our fragile social environments are under threat as well, slower in our culture, and also in our Catholic Church. It is therefore essential that we foster a new human ecology and advance it.

It is necessary first to promote the fundamental pillars that govern a nation: its nonmaterial goods. The family is the foundation of coexistence and a guarantee against social fragmentation. Children have a right to grow up in a family with a father and a mother capable of creating a suitable environment for the child's development and emotional maturity. That is why I stressed in the apostolic exhortation *Evangelii Gaudium* that the contribution of marriage to society is "indispensable"; that it "transcends the feelings and momentary needs of the couple" (n. 66). And that is why I am grateful to you for your Colloquium's emphasis on the benefits that marriage can provide to children, the spouses themselves, and to society.

In these days, as you embark on a reflection on the beauty of complementarity between man and woman in marriage, I urge you to lift up yet another truth about marriage: that permanent commitment to solidarity, fidelity, and fruitful love responds to the deepest longings of the human heart. Let us bear in mind especially the young people, who represent our future. It is important that they do not give themselves over to the poisonous mentality of the temporary, but rather be revolutionaries with the courage to seek true and lasting love, going against the common pattern.

With regard to this I want to say one thing: Let us not fall into the trap of being qualified by ideological concepts. Family is an anthropological fact – a socially and culturally related fact. We cannot qualify it with concepts of an ideological nature that are relevant only in a single moment of history and then pass by. We can't speak today of a conservative notion of family or a progressive notion of family. Family is family! It can't be qualified by ideological notions. Family has a strength in and of itself.

May this colloquium be an inspiration to all who seek to support and strengthen the union of man and woman in marriage as a unique, natural, fundamental, and beautiful good for persons, families, communities, and whole societies.

"This fact, indelible in human nature, reveals our radical dependence: we do not complete ourselves from our own selves, we are not totally self-sufficient."

GERHARD MÜLLER

2

GERHARD MÜLLER

An Opening to the Mystery of God

WE ARE GATHERED TO CONSIDER more deeply the theme of the complementarity between man and woman. Each of us, reflecting on his or her human condition, perceives how one's own humanity cannot be exhausted in oneself. One's own male or female being is not sufficient to oneself. Each one of us feels needy and lacking in completion. This fact, indelible in human nature, reveals our radical dependence: we do not complete ourselves from our own selves, we are not totally self-sufficient.

This simple consideration, clear to all, would suffice to demonstrate the inadequacy of the markedly individualistic trait so characteristic of the modern mentality. Yet in the roots of our "I," there is inscribed a natural tension, opposed to such a mentality, which is unfortunately now diffused in many parts of the world.

Our meeting takes as its point of departure this elementary consideration, opening it to the mystery of

God. It gives rise to the question: what import does the complementarity between man and woman have for the relationship between the human person and God? It is this question that each of our cultural and religious traditions is invited to engage.

From the Bible, an opening of perspective

In the Judeo-Christian perspective this theme is quite relevant and emerges immediately in the reading and interpretation found in tradition on the basis of some basic and essential biblical texts.

I begin with a passage from the Book of Proverbs, a collection of wisdom sayings of Israel: "Three things are too wonderful for me; four I do not understand: the way of an eagle in the sky, the way of a snake on a rock, the way of a ship on the high seas, and the way of a man with a maiden" (Prov. 30:18–19).

Here, proposed for our consideration, is a mystery of wisdom, which is relevant to the desire of all religions: to understand how God manifests himself in the world. The text offers three enigmas: the way of the eagle in the sky, the snake on the rock, the ship on the waters. To these three is added a fourth, according to a paradigm which,

---

✦ GERHARD CARDINAL MÜLLER *is prefect of the Congregation for the Doctrine of the Faith. In addition, he is president of the Pontifical Commission Ecclesia Dei, the Pontifical Biblical Commission, and the International Theological Commission. From 1986 to 2002, he was professor of dogmatic theology at Ludwig Maximilian University in Munich, Germany. He has also taught as a visiting professor at universities in Peru, the United States, India, Spain, Italy, Switzerland, and Brazil.*

in wisdom literature, represents the synthesis and fullness of the other three: "the way of a man with a maiden." It is well known that wisdom literature speaks of God, not directly, but from the point of view of his presence in, and action on, the created.

The first three enigmas gather all spheres of the cosmos: air, earth, water – in their movement from God and toward God. In this way, they bring to mind the first chapter of Genesis, which recounts the creation of all the elements of the cosmos and of all beings, following the temporal rhythm of the week toward the Sabbath rest in God. This account culminates in the creation of man and woman, inviting us in this way to consider the fourth enigma, "the way of a man with a maiden," as the fullness of all ways in which the Creator makes himself present in the created and propels it toward himself. In this sense, if the first account of creation finishes precisely on the Sabbath as the day of the covenant (Gen. 2:2–3), the second account finds its fulfilment in the appearance of man and woman, symbol of the great covenant between God and Israel (Gen. 2:22–24).

What then – in the light of this – is the meaning of the expression "the way of a man with a maiden"? According to some, it may refer to the path by which a man joins himself to a woman, to the conjugal union: the entire cosmos participates in the unity of one flesh between husband and wife, assumed in the body of the spouses, and opens itself in love toward the presence and action of God. The expression may also signify the path by which man and woman come out of themselves, that is to say birth as the marvelous locus for the presence of the Creator, who blesses his creature.

Hence, we may conclude that the difference between man and woman, both in the union of love and the generation of life, concerns God's presence in the world, which every person is called to discover in order to find a solid and lasting foundation and destiny for life.

The difference between man and woman as an essential element to understanding the human being and our journey toward God

These thoughts may assist us in the question which will be at the heart of our reflections during this gathering: in what way does God make himself present in the complementarity between man and woman? The response will be useful not only to draw closer to the divine mystery, but will also open us to a deeper understanding of the human person.

The presence of God appears in the first place in the way in which God models the body of man and woman. The Bible speaks of God as the artisan who shapes every person in the mother's womb (Jer. 1:5; Ps. 139:13). Faith in the Creator is linked to this initial experience: in the body, there exists a primordial language, a gift that enables us to receive and communicate love. The human body, in its sexual difference, is not a chance product of blind evolution or an anonymous determination of elements.

What is it that speaks to us of this difference contained in body language? This has attracted the attention of all cultures. For example, the myth of Androgyny, which Plato speaks about in his Symposium, is well known. By divine punishment, original man – a spherical being, and, at the same time, male and female, was divided in two in a way that each part remains in constant search of the other, in a continuous movement, thus blocking any representation of a threat to the gods.

The myth of Androgyny teaches us – just like the Bible in its account of Genesis – that sexual difference is not only diversity, in the same way that peoples and their customs are diverse, and does not merely signify a variegated plurality. Indeed, in itself plurality does not include the need of the other to understand itself, even if diversity may nevertheless be enriching. Rather, in sexual difference – and this is essential – each of the two can only understand himself or herself in light of the other: the male needs the female to be understood, and the same is true for the female. For this reason, the Bible puts Adam and Eve one before the other (Gen. 2:18). Difference thereby imbues in man and woman the knowledge that something is lacking in them, that they cannot find their fulfilment in themselves: each "only in communion with the opposite sex can become 'complete,'" as Benedict XVI wrote in the encyclical *Deus Caritas Est* (n. 11).

Hence, a different interpretation of this lack may be noted in the myth of Androgyny and in the Bible. Whereas in the first case, sexual difference is viewed as a punishment that weakens humans in order that they cannot draw near to the gods, thus becoming a fall from the almost divine level to impotent slavery, in the Bible difference is the place of blessing, the exact place where God will make present his action and his image.

In this way, we can comprehend that, while in the myth of Androgyny man and woman are two halves of a human being, in Scripture, each of the two, Adam and Eve, are measured not only according to their mutual relation but above all from the starting point of their relationship with God. Indeed, in the singularity of each and not only in their union as a couple, we find inscribed the image of the one who has created them. Here, man and woman share the same humanity, the same incarnate condition, and sexual difference does not imply subordination one to the other: "both man and woman are human beings to an equal degree, both are created in God's image" (*Mulieris Dignitatem,* n. 6). In this vein, Saint John Paul II said that male and female are as "two incarnations of the same metaphysical solitude before God and the world – two reciprocally completing ways of 'being a body' and at the same time of being human."

It is important to also underline another dissimilarity between the Platonic account and that of Scripture: whereas in the former, man and woman, when they unite, become a full and self-satisfied being, in the book of Genesis the union of man and woman does not lead to a fulfilment, does not close them within themselves, for it is precisely in uniting with each other that they open themselves to the greater presence of God. One might well say that in the very union of the two, man and woman render themselves needier, which increases in them the thirst of the mystery in the measure that their radical reference to the Creator God is revealed more clearly. The union sets off, therefore, a dynamic, a movement, as the Song of Songs recounts, in which the lover and beloved are at the same time in continuous search of the other and of God. Saint Augustine expressed this with magnificent words: "He created the one out of the other, setting a sign also of the power of the union in the side, whence she was drawn, was formed. For they are joined one to another side by side, who walk together, and look together whither they walk." For the Doctor from Hippo, this goal is none other than God himself.

It is precisely the presence of God within the union between man and woman that helps us consider the meaning of their complementarity. This cannot be understood in a polar fashion, as if male and female were opposed realities who complete each other perfectly (active and passive, exterior and interior, etc.) so as to become a closed unity; rather, it is a matter of different ways of situating themselves in the world so that, when they come together, far from closing themselves in, these open the path toward the world and others, a path that leads above all to the encounter with God. The union of male and female is complementary not in the sense that from it ensues one complete in himself or herself, but in the sense that their union demonstrates how both are a mutual help to journey toward the Creator.

The complementarity between man and woman in light of the mutual relationship with the child

The way in which this union refers to itself always beyond itself becomes evident in the birth of a child. The union of the two, making themselves "one flesh," is proven precisely in the one flesh of those generated by that union. Hence, we see confirmed how complementarity also means overabundance, an insurgence of novelty.

From the presence of the child comes a light that can help us describe the complementarity of man and woman. The relationship of the parents with the baby, where both open out beyond themselves, is a privileged way to understand the difference between the man and the woman in their role as father and mother. Complementarity is not understood, therefore, when we consider man and woman in an isolated form, but when we consider them from the perspective of the mystery to which their union opens out and, in a concrete way, when we look at male and female in light of the relationship with the child.

One might add that the female aspect is characterized by a constant presence, which always accompanies the child. Indeed, in German, when a woman is pregnant, we say that she "carries a baby beneath her heart" (*"dass sie ein Kind unter dem Herzen trägt"*). Contemporary philosophy has spoken of the feminine as a dwelling place, as presence that envelops us from the beginning and accompanies us along the way, as singular sensitivity for the person as gift and for our affirmation. On the other hand, the male is characterized, in terms of the child, as the presence of someone "in the distance," in a distance that attracts and, therefore, helps in walking the journey of life. Both male and female are necessary to transmit to the child the presence of the Creator, both as love that envelops and confirms the goodness of existence despite all else, and as a call that from afar invites one to grow. In this way, male and female are dimensions that interconnect and exchange, such that the woman enriches man and man the woman, because one participates in the property of the other and together they may transmit to the child what it means to be the image of God.

From what I have said above, there emerges an important consequence: the first place where sexual difference appears in the life of a person is exactly in the experience of offspring. Our origin, our first place of contact with the mystery, is revealed in the union of our parents from which comes life. Male and female make visible for each child who comes into the world, in a sacramental way, the presence of the Creator. The good of this difference, the perception of male and female, is the essential grammar to educate the child as a person open to the mystery of God.

For this reason, when sexual difference is not integrated in one's life – a task that is carried out laboriously and requires effort and time in openness to others – it is impossible to clarify and accept one's own identity; it is impossible to find the path of life. This opens up a terrain for the merciful action of the church, and of all religions, toward persons who have been injured.

The complementarity of man and woman, from this point of view, contains an essential social role; we are dealing with a common good that society is called to protect so as to promote the common good. Without being able to enumerate every aspect of this richness, we may say that sexual difference is a good for society insofar as it guarantees the dignity of the person who is born, who will never be – when generated within the conjugal union – the product of the isolated wish of an individual, but the fruit, always overflowing, of a spousal love that opens itself to the mystery. Complementarity becomes essential in the generation and upbringing of the child and, hence, in the journey of society through time, in the essential link that exists through all generations.

Complementarity: an essential task for the religious person

The complementarity of man and woman, therefore, carries with itself a great treasure of humanity, because it enables persons to be defined in their deepest nature by a relationship of love, and to give this bond a generative relationship that welcomes the gift of a new person. In this way, it helps us understand the divine mystery that reveals itself therein and which Jesus confirmed, speaking of the union between a man and woman as "that which God has united" (Matt. 19:6).

We can understand then, precisely why God chose the difference between man and woman to manifest his love story with the people of Israel. When the richness of sexual difference is not welcomed, it is impossible to understand the fidelity of God as spouse, who continually forgives Israel her infidelities. We can also understand why Christ assumed this language of male and female – transforming it in line with the virginal novelty of his life – to express the fullness of charity. Without this language, without the experience of the goodness of sexual difference, it would be impossible to grasp the work of God, his love for us, and the way in which he loves us and uses mercy towards us. Precisely on the basis of the relationships that are born around "one flesh" of man and woman, God reveals his mercy, comparing it to the father who forgives the son (Hosea 11:1–8; Luke 15:11–24), to the mother who does not abandon her child (Isa. 49:14–15), and the spouse who welcomes again the unfaithful wife (Hosea 2:20; John 8:1–10).

The task of this meeting will be to explore the richness of sexual difference, its goodness, its character as gift, its openness to life, and the path that it opens up to God. As our Holy Father, Pope Francis, writes in his encyclical *Lumen Fidei:*

> The first setting in which faith enlightens the human city is the family. I think first and foremost of the stable

union of man and woman in marriage. This union is born of their love, as a sign and presence of God's own love, and of the acknowledgment and acceptance of the goodness of sexual differentiation, whereby spouses can become one flesh (Gen. 2:24) and are enabled to give birth to a new life, a manifestation of the Creator's goodness, wisdom, and loving plan. (n. 52)

"When a man and woman turn to one another in a bond of faithfulness, God robes them in garments of light, and we come as close as we will ever get to God himself, bringing new life into being, turning the prose of biology into the poetry of the human spirit, redeeming the darkness of the world by the radiance of love."

JONATHAN SACKS

3

JONATHAN SACKS

Seven Key Moments in History

A Jewish Perspective

I WANT TO BEGIN OUR conversation by telling the story of the most beautiful idea in the history of civilization: the idea of the love that brings new life into the world. There are of course many ways of telling the story, and this is just one. But to me it is a story of seven key moments, each of them surprising and unexpected. The first, according to a report in the press on October 20, 2014, took place in a lake in Scotland 385 million years ago. It was then, according to this new discovery, that two fish came together to perform the first instance of sexual reproduction known to science. Until then all life had propagated itself asexually, by cell division, budding, fragmentation, or parthenogenesis, all of which are far simpler and more economical than the division of life into male and female, each with a different role in creating and sustaining life.

When we consider, even in the animal kingdom, how much effort and energy the coming together of male and female takes, in terms of displays, courtship rituals, rivalries, and violence, it is astonishing that sexual reproduction ever happened at all. Biologists are still not quite sure why it did. Some say to offer protection against parasites, or immunities against disease. Others say it's simply that the meeting of opposites generates diversity. But one way or another, the fish in Scotland discovered something new and beautiful that's been copied ever since by virtually all advanced forms of life. Life begins when male and female meet and embrace.

The second unexpected development was the unique challenge posed to *Homo sapiens* by two factors: we stood upright, which constricted the female pelvis, and we had bigger brains – a 300 percent increase – which meant larger heads. The result was that human babies had to be born more prematurely than any other species, and so needed parental protection for much longer. This made parenting more demanding among humans than any other species, the work of two people rather than one. Hence the very rare phenomenon among mammals, of pair bonding, unlike other species where the male

---

✦ RABBI LORD JONATHAN SACKS *is the former chief rabbi of the United Kingdom and the Commonwealth. Rabbi Sacks is currently the Ingeborg and Ira Rennert Global Distinguished Professor of Judaic Thought at New York University and the Kressel and Ephrat Family University Professor of Jewish Thought at Yeshiva University. He has also been appointed as Professor of Law, Ethics, and the Bible at King's College, London. He was knighted by Queen Elizabeth in 2005 and made a life peer in the House of Lords in October 2009.*

contribution tends to end with the act of impregnation. Among most primates, fathers don't even recognize their children let alone care for them. Elsewhere in the animal kingdom motherhood is almost universal but fatherhood is rare.

So what emerged along with the human person was the union of the biological mother and father to care for their child. Thus far nature, but then came culture, and the third surprise.

It seems that among hunter-gatherers pair bonding was the norm. Then came agriculture, and economic surplus, and cities and civilization, and for the first time sharp inequalities began to emerge between rich and poor, powerful and powerless. The great ziggurats of Mesopotamia and pyramids of ancient Egypt, with their broad base and narrow top, were monumental statements in stone of a hierarchical society in which the few had power over the many. And the most obvious expression of power among alpha males, whether human or primate, is to dominate access to fertile women and thus maximize the handing on of your genes to the next generation. Hence polygamy, which exists in ninety-five percent of mammal species and seventy-five percent of cultures known to anthropology. Polygamy is the ultimate expression of inequality because it means that many males never get the chance to have a wife and child. And sexual envy has been, throughout history, among animals as well as humans, a prime driver of violence.

That is what makes the first chapter of Genesis so revolutionary with its statement that every human being, regardless of class, color, culture, or creed, is in the image and likeness of God himself. We know that in the ancient world it was rulers, kings, emperors, and pharaohs who were held to be in the image of God. So what Genesis was saying was that we are all royalty. We each have equal dignity in the kingdom of faith under the sovereignty of God.

From this it follows that we each have an equal right to form a marriage and have children, which is why, regardless of how we read the story of Adam and Eve – and there are differences between Jewish and Christian readings – the norm presupposed by that story is: one woman, one man. Or as the Bible itself says: "That is why a man leaves his father and mother and is united to his wife, and they become one flesh."

Monogamy did not immediately become the norm, even within the world of the Bible. But many of its most famous stories, about the tension between Sarah and Hagar, or Leah and Rachel and their children, or David and Bathsheba, or Solomon's many wives, are all critiques that point the way to monogamy.

And there is a deep connection between monotheism and monogamy, just as there is, in the opposite direction, between idolatry and adultery. Monotheism and monogamy are about the all-embracing relationship between I and Thou, myself and one other, be it a human other or the divine Other.

What makes the emergence of monogamy unusual is that it is normally the case that the values of a society are those imposed on it by the ruling class. And the ruling class in any hierarchical society stands to gain from promiscuity and polygamy, both of which multiply the chances of the ruling elites' genes being handed on to the next generation. From monogamy the rich and powerful

lose and the poor and powerless gain. So the return of monogamy goes against the normal grain of social change and was a real triumph for the equal dignity of all. Every bride and every groom are royalty; every home a palace when furnished with love.

The fourth remarkable development was the way this transformed the moral life. We've all become familiar with the work of evolutionary biologists using computer simulations and the iterated prisoners' dilemma to explain why reciprocal altruism exists among all social animals. We behave to others as we would wish them to behave to us, and we respond to them as they respond to us. As C. S. Lewis pointed out in his book *The Abolition of Man,* reciprocity is the Golden Rule shared by all the great civilizations.

What was new and remarkable in the Hebrew Bible was the idea that love, not just fairness, is the driving principle of the moral life. Three loves. "Love the Lord your God with all your heart, all your soul, and all your might." "Love your neighbor as yourself." And, repeated no less than thirty-six times in the Mosaic books, "Love the stranger because you know what it feels like to be a stranger." Or to put it another way: just as God created the natural world in love and forgiveness, so we are charged with creating the social world in love and forgiveness. And that love is a flame lit in marriage and the family. Morality is the love between husband and wife, parent and child, extended outward to the world.

The fifth development shaped the entire structure of Jewish experience. In ancient Israel an originally secular form of agreement, called a covenant, was taken and transformed into a new way of thinking about the relationship between God and humanity, in the case of Noah, and between God and a people in the case of Abraham and later the Israelites at Mount Sinai. A covenant is like a marriage. It is a mutual pledge of loyalty and trust between two or more people, each respecting the dignity and integrity of the other, to work together to achieve together what neither can achieve alone. And there is one thing even God cannot achieve alone, which is to live within the human heart. That needs us.

So the Hebrew word *emunah,* wrongly translated as faith, really means faithfulness, fidelity, loyalty, steadfastness, not walking away even when the going gets tough, trusting the other and honoring the other's trust in us. What covenant did, and we see this in almost all the prophets, was to understand the relationship between us and God in terms of the relationship between bride and groom, wife and husband. Love thus became not only the basis of morality but also of theology. In Judaism faith is a marriage. Rarely was this more beautifully stated than by Hosea when he said in the name of God:

> I will betroth you to me forever; I will betroth you in righteousness and justice, love and compassion. I will betroth you in faithfulness, and you will know the Lord.

Jewish men say those words every weekday morning as we wind the strap of our tefillin around our finger like a wedding ring. Each morning we renew our marriage with God.

This led to a sixth and quite subtle idea: that truth, beauty, goodness, and life itself do not exist in any one person or entity but in the "between," what Martin Buber called *das Zwischenmenschliche,* the interpersonal, the counterpoint of speaking and listening, giving and receiving. Throughout the Hebrew Bible and the rabbinic literature, the vehicle of truth is conversation. In revelation God speaks and asks us to listen. In prayer we speak and ask God to listen. There is never only one voice. In the Bible the prophets argue with God. In the Talmud rabbis argue with one another. In fact I sometimes think the reason God chose the Jewish people was because he loves a good argument. Judaism is a conversation scored for many voices, never more passionately than in the Song of Songs, a duet between a woman and a man, the beloved and her lover, that Rabbi Akiva called the holy of holies of religious literature.

The prophet Malachi calls the male priest the guardian of the law of truth. The book of Proverbs says of the woman of worth that "the law of loving kindness is on her tongue." It is that conversation between male and female voices, between truth and love, justice and mercy, law and forgiveness, that frames the spiritual life. In biblical times each Jew had to give a half shekel to the Temple to remind us that we are only half. There are some cultures that teach that we are nothing. There are others that teach that we are everything. The Jewish view is that we are half and we need to open ourselves to another if we are to become whole.

All this led to the seventh outcome, that in Judaism the home and the family became the central setting of the life of faith. In the only verse in the Hebrew Bible to explain why God chose Abraham, he says: "I have known him so that he will instruct his children and his household after him to keep the way of the Lord by doing what is right and just." Abraham was chosen not to rule an empire, command an army, perform miracles, or deliver prophecies, but simply to be a parent. In one of the most famous lines in Judaism, which we say every day and night, Moses commands: "You shall teach these things repeatedly to your children, speaking of them when you sit in your house or when you walk on the way, when you lie down and when you rise up." Parents are to be educators, education is the conversation between the generations, and the first school is the home.

So Jews became an intensely family oriented people, and it was this that saved us from tragedy. After the destruction of the Second Temple in the year AD 70, Jews were scattered throughout the world, everywhere a minority, everywhere without rights, suffering some of the worst persecutions ever known by a people. And yet Jews survived because they never lost three things: their sense of family, their sense of community, and their faith.

And they were renewed every week especially on Shabbat, the day of rest when we give our marriages and families what they most need and are most starved of in the contemporary world, namely time.

I once produced a television documentary for the BBC on the state of family life in Britain, and I took the person who was then Britain's leading expert on child care, Penelope Leach, to a Jewish primary school on a Friday morning.

There she saw the children enacting in advance what they would see that evening around the family table. There were the five-year-old mother and father blessing the five-year-old children with the five-year-old grandparents looking on. She was fascinated by this whole institution, and she asked the children what they most enjoyed about the Sabbath. One five-year-old boy turned to her and said, "It's the only night of the week when daddy doesn't have to rush off." As we walked away from the school when the filming was over she turned to me and said, "Chief Rabbi, that Sabbath of yours is saving their parents' marriages."

So that is one way of telling the story, a Jewish way, beginning with the birth of sexual reproduction, then the unique demands of human parenting, then the eventual triumph of monogamy as a fundamental statement of human equality, followed by the way marriage shaped our vision of the moral and religious life as based on love and covenant and faithfulness, even to the point of thinking of truth as a conversation between lover and beloved. Marriage and the family are where faith finds its home and where the Divine Presence lives in the love between husband and wife, parent and child.

What then has changed? Here's one way of putting it. I wrote a book a few years ago about religion and science and I summarized the difference between them in two sentences. "Science takes things apart to see how they work. Religion puts things together to see what they mean." And that's a way of thinking about culture also. Does it put things together or does it take things apart?

What made the traditional family remarkable, a work of high religious art, is what it brought together: sexual drive, physical desire, friendship, companionship, emotional kinship and love, the begetting of children and their protection and care, their early education and induction into an identity and a history. Seldom has any institution woven together so many different drives and desires, roles and responsibilities. It made sense of the world and gave it a human face, the face of love.

For a whole variety of reasons – some to do with medical developments like birth control, in vitro fertilization and other genetic interventions, some to do with moral change like the idea that we are free to do whatever we like so long as it does not harm others, some to do with a transfer of responsibilities from the individual to the state, and other and more profound changes in the culture of the West – almost everything that marriage once brought together has now been split apart. Sex has been divorced from love, love from commitment, marriage from having children, and having children from responsibility for their care.

The result is that in Britain in 2012, 47.5 percent of children were born outside marriage, expected to become a majority in 2016. Fewer people are marrying, those who are, are marrying later, and forty-two percent of marriages end in divorce. Nor is cohabitation a substitute for marriage. The average length of cohabitation in Britain and the United States is less than two years. The result is a sharp increase among young people of eating disorders, drug and alcohol abuse, stress related syndromes, depression, and actual and attempted suicides. The collapse of marriage has created a new form of poverty concentrated among single parent families, and of these, the main burden is borne by women, who in 2011 headed 92 percent of single parent households. In Britain today more than a million children will grow up with no contact whatsoever with their fathers.

This is creating a divide within societies the like of which has not been seen since Disraeli spoke of "two nations" a century and a half ago. Those who are privileged to grow up in stable, loving association with the two people who brought them into being will, on average, be healthier physically and emotionally. They will do better at school and at work. They will have more successful relationships, be happier, and live longer. And yes, there are many exceptions. But the injustice of it all cries out to heaven. It will go down in history as one of the tragic instances of what Friedrich Hayek called "the fatal conceit" that somehow we know better than the wisdom of the ages, and can defy the lessons of biology and history.

No one, surely, wants to go back to the narrow prejudices of the past. Recently, in Britain, a new film opened, telling the story of one of the great minds of the twentieth century, Alan Turing, the Cambridge mathematician who laid the philosophical foundations of computing and artificial intelligence, and helped win the war by breaking the German naval code Enigma. After the war, Turing was arrested and tried for homosexual behavior, underwent chemically induced castration, and died at the age of forty-one by cyanide poisoning, thought by many to have committed suicide. That is a world to which we should never return.

But our compassion for those who choose to live differently should not inhibit us from being advocates for the single most humanizing institution in history. The family – man, woman, and child – is not one lifestyle choice among many. It is the best means we have yet discovered for nurturing future generations and enabling children to grow in a matrix of stability and love. It is where we learn the delicate choreography of relationship and how to handle the inevitable conflicts within any human group. It is where we first take the risk of giving and receiving love. It is where one generation passes on its values to the next, ensuring the continuity of a civilization. For any society, the family is the crucible of its future, and for the sake of our children's future, we must be its defenders.

Since this is a religious gathering, let me, if I may, end with a piece of biblical exegesis. The story of the first family, the first man and woman in the Garden of Eden, is not generally regarded as a success. Whether or not we believe in original sin, it did not end happily. After many years of studying the text I want to suggest a different reading.

The story ends with three verses that seem to have no connection with one another. No sequence. No logic. In Genesis 3:19 God says to the man: "By the sweat of your brow you will eat your food until you return to the ground, since from it you were taken; for dust you are and to dust you will return." Then in the next verse we read: "The man named his wife Eve, because she was the mother of all life." And in the next, "The Lord God made garments of skin for Adam and his wife and clothed them."

What is the connection here? Why did God telling the man that he was mortal lead him to give his wife a new name? And why did that act seem to change God's attitude to both of them, so that he performed an act of tenderness, by making them clothes, almost as if he had partially forgiven them? Let me also add that the Hebrew word for "skin" is almost indistinguishable from the Hebrew word for "light," so that Rabbi Meir, the great sage of the early second century, read the text as saying that God made for them "garments of light." What did he mean?

If we read the text carefully, we see that until now the first man had given his wife a purely generic name. He called her *ishah,* woman. Recall what he said when he first saw her: "This is now bone of my bones and flesh of my flesh; she shall be called woman for she was taken from man." For him she was a type, not a person. He gave her a noun, not a name. What is more, he defines her as a derivative of himself: something taken from man. She is not yet for him someone other, a person in her own right. She is merely a reflection of himself.

As long as the man thought he was immortal, he ultimately needed no one else. But now he knew he was mortal. He would one day die and return to dust. There was only one way in which something of him would live on after his death. That would be if he had a child. But he could not have a child on his own. For that he needed his wife. She alone could give birth. She alone could mitigate his mortality. And not because she was like him but precisely because she was unlike him. At that moment she ceased to be, for him, a type, and became a person in her own right. And a person has a proper name. That is what he gave her: the name *Chavvah,* "Eve," meaning, "giver of life."

At that moment, as they were about to leave Eden and face the world as we know it, a place of darkness, Adam gave his wife the first gift of love, a personal name. And at that moment, God responded to them both in love, and made them garments to clothe their nakedness, or as Rabbi Meir put it, "garments of light."

And so it has been ever since, that when a man and woman turn to one another in a bond of faithfulness, God robes them in garments of light, and we come as close as we will ever get to God himself, bringing new life into being, turning the prose of biology into the poetry of the human spirit, redeeming the darkness of the world by the radiance of love.

"Marriage is more than a private contract between two people. God did not have in mind merely the personal happiness of separate individuals, but the establishment of God-fearing relationships in a communion of families under his rulership."

JOHANN CHRISTOPH ARNOLD

4

JOHANN CHRISTOPH ARNOLD

A Living Witness for Marriage

An Anabaptist Perspective

WHAT A JOY IT IS to be here with all of you to celebrate and proclaim the treasure of God-given marriage – a plan that is as perfect today as it was in the beginning: one man, one woman, for life.

This gathering gives me so much hope and shows the importance of giving living witness to God's design for marriage. Children and young people desperately need to see role models who prove with their lives that faithful marriage is one of the most wonderful ways one can serve humankind.

But married couples standing alone aren't enough. We need strong faith communities to sustain and support them.

My wife, Verena, and I have experienced this during forty-eight years of marriage. At our wedding we made vows of lifelong faithfulness, with Jesus Christ as the foundation of our marriage, that have been used in the Anabaptist church for nearly five hundred years. We received the blessing from the God of Abraham, of Isaac, and of Jacob that has been handed down for thousands of years. God really blessed us! We have eight children, forty-four grandchildren, and two great-grandchildren!

Last year my wife was diagnosed with a serious cancer and more recently she suffered a heart attack. It seemed that the devil tried everything to prevent us from coming to Rome but, praise God, we are here today.

I share this because we are just like everybody else, with our struggles and challenges, and have come to understand how important it is to belong to a community of believers that protects the values that sustain marriage. This is true in the Bruderhof, the church community that I come from, and it is so in all the great faith traditions that are here today. This is why I have hope that marriage as God intended it will shine forth even in these dark times.

WE LIVE IN TUMULTUOUS TIMES. The same was true in 1920, when my grandparents, Eberhard and Emmy

---

✦ JOHANN CHRISTOPH ARNOLD *is a senior pastor of the Bruderhof, an international communal movement dedicated to a life of simplicity, service, sharing, and nonviolence. In forty years of pastoral experience, Arnold has advised thousands of couples and individuals, including the terminally ill, veterans, prison inmates, and teenagers. He is an award-winning author with over a million copies of his books in print, in more than twenty languages, among them* Why Children Matter *and* Sex, God, and Marriage. *He and his wife, Verena, have eight children.*

Arnold, began a small community in Germany based on Jesus' teachings and inspired by the witness of the early Christians. They banded together as singles and married couples to live a life of complete sharing as described in the Book of Acts. That humble beginning has grown to twenty-five Bruderhof communities on four continents.

While serving as elder of this movement for the last thirty years, I've watched the moral and spiritual decline of Western civilization, along with the tragic breakdown of the family. All the more, we have been determined to uphold the sanctity of life, and of sex and marriage.

We believe that marriage is more than a private contract between two people. God did not have in mind merely the personal happiness of separate individuals, but the establishment of God-fearing relationships in a communion of families under his rulership. Marriage is part of God's original creation and sanctifies each generation as being "made in the image of God." God created male and female that through their union they might fill the earth and flourish. In God's plan, every child has a father and a mother.

AS A PASTORAL TEAM, my wife and I have seen that a marriage is vulnerable without a fellowship of believers who seek each other out for strength, support, and advice. If we want strong marriages we need to build faithful communities dedicated to living out Jesus' teachings of chastity, forgiveness, and sharing. This means couples as well as single men and women who demonstrate what it means to be true disciples of God.

This is not easy. Our human nature too easily gives in to sinful desires. Yet the selfishness which leads to infidelity and divorce can be overcome through Jesus and his Spirit. What God joins together can remain together. Through Jesus, the walls of bitterness, blame, and selfish ambition that divide us can be torn down.

In my own church community, there are people from all walks of life, including some from very broken families. Like couples everywhere, couples in our church have to work hard to nurture the kind of love that truly lasts. Sometimes they find themselves in crisis due to mistrust, unforgiveness, or sexual immorality. But through the help of God and of fellow church members, miracles of reconciliation and healing can and do happen. Prayer is a crucial part of this process: as the old saying goes, "Couples that pray together, stay together."

To protect marriages, we as individuals, families, and churches must hold each other accountable and encourage each other. Our children need to see a life of modesty, simplicity, hard work, and most of all love to God and neighbor.

OF COURSE, God's plan will not always be welcomed. In 1995 I sent my first book, *Sex, God, and Marriage,* to my dear friend Cardinal Joseph Ratzinger, now Pope Emeritus. He presented it to Pope John Paul II and wrote this in response:

> I was glad to deliver *Sex, God, and Marriage* to the Holy Father. He was very happy for this ecumenical gesture and, more than that, for the content, and for the harmony of the moral conviction that springs from our common faith in Christ. Such conviction will inevitably arouse hatred, and even persecution. The Lord has predicted it. But with him we must continue in trying to overcome evil through good.

These words have proven to be prophetic, as sadly this hatred and persecution has now started. Today, lifelong marriage between one man and one woman is being rejected and those who uphold it are scorned. Yet we must continue to defend marriage for our children.

The family is the bedrock for the survival of the human race. We must remain faithful and encourage one another, as we are doing today. I thank God that our brother Pope Francis is continuing to do this in the "harmony of moral conviction that springs from our common faith in Christ." Let us remember Jesus' words: "Where two or three are gathered in my name, there I will be also" (Matt. 18:20).

The false teachings about marriage cannot be reversed by words alone. Children and young people need to see God's love and truth in action. I experienced this through the example of my parents, who faced incredible obstacles during their forty-six years of marriage. But they never wavered. Through their love to Jesus they had their sights set on God's kingdom right to the end of their lives.

Such examples are needed today. Like the early church we need to become more courageous – a counterculture of simplicity and practical help where we dedicate our entire energy to building up God's kingdom, not to chasing after the things of this world. The first Christians turned the Roman world upside down partly because husbands and wives remained faithful to one another and to their children – something the pagans did not think was possible. With God's help, we too can do the same today.

We must never be afraid of the ridicule and slander our witness will bring. As the apostle Paul wrote:

> Do not be deceived: God cannot be mocked. A man reaps what he sows. Whoever sows to please their flesh, from the flesh will reap destruction; whoever sows to please the Spirit, from the Spirit will reap eternal life. Let us not become weary in doing good, for at the proper time we will reap a harvest if we do not give up. (Gal. 6:7–9)

So, let us hold our heads high knowing that if God is for us, who can be against us? Let us give living witness together that God's plan for marriage and children is joyful, true, and everlasting. Nothing will be able to stop us from proclaiming this childlike and simple message. It is God who holds the final hour of history in his hands, and he will be victorious.

"In the Arabic language and the Qur'an, 'husband,' 'wife,' and 'married couple' are all indicated by the same word, zawj, *which means 'two persons, different from one another, bound together, who cannot manage without each other.'"*

WAEL FAROUQ

5

WAEL FAROUQ

We Exist in Relationship

A Muslim Perspective

"*BI-SMI-LLÀH AL-RAHMÀN AL-RAHÌM,* in the name of God, the Most Beneficent, the Most Merciful." Muslims do not undertake any action in their daily life without first pronouncing this sentence. The same sentence precedes all the suras in the Noble Qur'an. *Al-Rahìm* (the Most Merciful) is the name of God and *rahma* (mercy, compassion) is his attribute. *Rahma,* in the Noble Qur'an, is referred to 268 times, both in the form of noun and verb, with different meanings.

The word *rahma* carries the meanings of kindliness, affection, grace, pardon, recompense, fulfillment of a prayer, rain, and paradise. The meaning of *rahma* garners all that is good and useful to the human being, in this world and in the afterworld. Hardly any issue dealt with by the Qur'an is driven by, or targeted at, something other than *rahma*. If it were possible to replace the Islamic religion with one word, it would be the word *rahma*, and the name of Islam would be "the religion of *rahma*." God Almighty says: "We sent thee not, save as a mercy for the peoples" (Qur'an 21:107). This is why the Islamic jurists have all agreed that what departs from *rahma* is not from the sharia.

This crucial word, *rahma*, and its essential meaning both derive from *rahim*, the woman's womb. The word *rahim* also means kinship and family ties, about which God Almighty says, in an oral tradition, "The one who fastens them, I will fasten him to me; the one who cuts them, I will cut him from me." Thus, the family is the manifestation of God's presence and love for us, our means to get closer to him and be completed in him. The womb, like the heart, is a source of life and meaning. For this reason, I can define the complementarity of man and woman as an encounter that generates life and meaning. With life and meaning, here, I do not refer only to children, who may be born or not, but also to a life that acquires meaning, and to a meaning that comes to life, in every encounter between a man and a woman.

I say this while I am feeling humiliated. For, while I am standing here among you bearing witness to this faith, ferocious crimes are being committed in its name

---

✦ WAEL FAROUQ *is a visiting professor at Catholic University of Milano. Born in Cairo, Egypt, Professor Farouq was previously a fellow at The Straus Institute for the Advanced Study of Law & Justice at New York University and assistant professor for Islamic studies at the Copto-Catholic Faculty of Theology in Cairo. He has been a visiting professor at Macerata University since 2005 and an instructor at the American University in Cairo since 2006. He is a columnist in several Arab and Italian newspapers and magazines as well as president of the Tawasul Cultural Center for Inter-civilization Dialogue.*

in Iraq and Syria. My only consolation is the testimony that those helpless believers are offering us in front of this evil, because the Iraqi victims did not succumb to a natural catastrophe, but were confronted with a choice, and they chose. Only a few words would have sufficed to disavow their faith and avoid all those pains, but instead they chose to keep their faith and leave everything else. They chose a life immersed in pain, but full of meaning. The people who made this heroic decision are not extraordinary, but were confronted in an extraordinarily dramatic moment with the question: Who am I? What is essential to my life? What is connecting the fugacious moment I am living with its eternal meaning?

Many of us spend most of our lives without facing those questions, because in our contemporary human culture the ephemeral has become central. We have ephemeral lives, ephemeral jobs, ephemeral relationships, ephemeral marriages, and ephemeral dwellings. All the things we use in our daily life are ephemeral as well: paper tissues, plastic bags, plastic dishes and cutlery, etc. Nothing carries a distinguishing sign, nothing carries a meaning, because everything is transient. Thus, the attention of contemporary culture has shifted from "being" in the world to "becoming" or passing across the world. Ours is indeed the world of the ephemeral and transitory. Ideologies have fallen, but the fear of the other has increased. Nihilism has withdrawn, but its place has been taken by passive neutrality toward everything. The prefix "post-" that introduces all aspects of human knowledge (post-industrialism, post-history, post-colonialism, post-modernism, etc.) implies the incapacity of conferring meaning on the present human condition. The German philosopher Jürgen Habermas sees in this situation a consequence of religion's exclusion from public life. As a matter of fact, all social challenges we have to face in our societies are essentially connected with the incapacity of giving life a meaning, and religion is certainly considered as one of the main sources of meaning.

Post-modernists believe that they have freed humanity from intellectual dichotomies such as good and evil, presence and absence, I and the Other. However, they just passed from the opposition between the elements of these dichotomies – and the ensuing capacity of pronouncing judgments that reflect, as a whole, a culture and an individual as well as collective identity – to a leveling of all those elements, from which ensues the incapacity of pronouncing judgments and, consequently, the interruption of any interaction with reality. This eventually leads to the standardization of both the individual and collective identity.

Post-modernism has fought against the "exclusion" carried out by modernism at the expense of the "different," but hasn't found a better way to do it than by excluding "difference" itself. Undoubtedly, the most serious danger that family faces today is its deprivation of meaning, the enlargement of its boundaries to the point of explosion and fragmentation, the eradication of its historical and human context, and its transformation into something we possess, buy, and sell. Family has become a consumer good. The so-called "new rights" treat family as merchandise that everybody has the right to consume, as long as they can afford it.

This is what makes the testimony of Iraqi Christians the greatest testimony of faith in our contemporary world. For we do need something that shakes our conscience in order to understand that we are in front of the same challenge those Iraqi people are facing and the same choice they are confronted with, that is to say, to live a life full of meaning. What we need is only to rediscover the truths of our culture and reformulate them in such a way that they harmonize with our contemporary world.

The Arabic language does not have an auxiliary verb "to be." Consequently, a single word acquires meaning or a grammatical function only within a sentence or, in other words, in a relationship with other words. A word in a sentence is exactly like an individual in a family. An individual does not "exist" outside a relationship. He is a brother in his relationship with his sister, a father in his relationship with his daughter, a son in his relationship with his mother, a husband in his relationship with his wife (and the same holds for a female, of course). In the Arabic language and the Qur'an alike (Qur'an 4:1; 7:189; 39:6), "husband," "wife," and "married couple" are all indicated by the same word, *zawj,* which means "two persons, different from one another, bound together, who cannot manage without each other." Therefore, marriage is not only a legal frame for a sexual relationship. It is a form of existence, an experience of mutual completion, a space for the emergence of God's love and his compassion for the world. God Almighty says, "And of His signs is this: He created for you helpmeets for yourselves that ye might find rest in them, and He ordained between you love and mercy" (Qur'an 30:21). Thus, both in the Arabic language and the Qur'an, the man and woman exist, but they cannot be unless they are in a relationship. This idea is rooted in Arabic culture. In the desert, in fact, the worst punishment was not death but the expulsion from the tribe, because outside the tribe a person exists but cannot be. Likewise, a person exists but cannot be unless he or she is in a relationship with someone else.

Unlimited freedom, which is regarded as an absolute value in our contemporary culture, remains blind when it is not embodied in an "unlimited being," or if it is not – as Luigi Giussani said – an emotional force that leads to God. This unlimited freedom, as it is lived today, does not build bridges. That is why, in the age of the communications revolution, we live as separate islands. Meanwhile, people assume that the simple existence of a person's desire for something gives this person the right to strive for its fulfillment. The right to consume has become the criterion of reference for all other rights, so that we keep reducing our humanity to what is transient and ephemeral.

The question now is: How do we face this reality, not just in extraordinarily dramatic moments but in our daily lives? The answer to this question might be found in the following story.

A young man met a girl at university and they became friends. They shared many interests: the study, the food, a love of arts, and other things. With the strengthening of their friendship, the girl was becoming tenser and tenser, until one day she told him nervously: "I am a lesbian." To which the boy replied: "But are you only this?" He didn't judge her morally, contrary to what she was expecting. He didn't feel morally superior to her. He simply behaved as a friend who loves his friend. The proverb says that love is blind, because it doesn't see the faults of the beloved. In my opinion, love is discernment, because it can see what lies behind. What did that boy see? He saw a "being" much greater than a choice that might change. Unlike the girl, the boy didn't reduce her existence to her sexual activity. He simply loved her, and the one who loves is able to see. Pope Benedict XVI said, "We do not possess truth, we are possessed by truth." Those who possess the truth judge and condemn others, whereas those who are possessed by truth cannot do anything else but to bear witness to it, and they know no other way to do this than to love.

Faced with a dominant discourse that considers children as objects that adults have the right to possess, we could get angry or take legal recourse to prevent this crime. However, our anger and resistance could easily hide the fact that we too are contributing to the formulation of this discourse, for when I say, "I have a child," I turn that child into an object I can possess. Moreover, the worst thing in that sentence is that it denies my personal experience, the truth and the reality I am living: that I actually am a father. I do not "have a child," but "I am a father."

Those who possess the truth choose only once in their life. Those who are possessed by truth, on the other hand, are challenged by choice every single day, because with every choice they make, their unique "being" takes shape, bearing witness to a truth which far exceeds the transient and the ephemeral; a truth bred in a womb that is pulsating with love inside every man and woman: the heart.

The choice I am speaking about is not a way to escape confrontation. On the contrary, it is the hardest way to follow. Still, let's always remember that the deepest darkness is not able to dim even the weakest ray of a single candle.

"We are most fortunate to live in a time of history when many important truths revealed in Scripture about the integral complementarity of woman and man have been verified by science and philosophy. . . . There is no excuse left to defend anything other than the equal dignity and significant difference of women and men."

M. PRUDENCE ALLEN

6

M. PRUDENCE ALLEN

Four Principles of Complementarity

A Philosophical Perspective

IN THIS BRIEF PRESENTATION I will develop the following points: One, the four principles of complementarity are revealed in Genesis. Two, gender reality includes sex identity. Three, sex and gender ideologies distort the truth about the relation of woman and man. Four, complementarity flourishes on a true metaphysical foundation.

The four principles of complementarity are revealed in Genesis.

The four principles of complementarity are: equal dignity, significant difference, synergetic relation, and intergenerational fruition. The marriage of one woman and one man is the prime model for all other kinds of complementarity in the world. When they live their complementarity integrally, respecting each other's equal dignity and significant differences, then their relation is synergetic. A simple way to summarize synergy is to say that one plus one becomes three. In other words, it becomes something more than just two independent persons living next to one another. When the synergy of a married woman and man with the grace of God generates another human being, their complementarity becomes inter-generational; it flourishes generation after generation.

The Book of Genesis reveals these four principles through revelation and faith. The principle of the equal dignity of all human beings is revealed in Genesis 1:26: "Let us make man [the human being] in our image, after our likeness." The significant difference between a woman and a man is revealed in Genesis 1:27: ". . . in the image of God he created them; male and female he created them." The synergetic relation of a woman and a man is revealed in Genesis 1:28: "And God blessed them, and God said to them, 'be fruitful and multiply' . . ." and in Genesis 2:24 ". . . they became one flesh."

The fourth principle of intergenerational fruition is revealed in Genesis 5:1–32: "This is the book of the generations" and in the subsequent listing of those who generated one generation after another from Adam

---

✦ SR. M. PRUDENCE ALLEN, PHD, *of the Religious Sisters of Mercy of Alma, is the author of a study titled "The Concept of Woman," tracing the understanding of woman in relation to man in the work of more than seventy philosophers through the ages. She has done extensive research on the development of feminism throughout history and has authored numerous scholarly articles on theological and philosophical themes. She was instrumental in the formation of Endow, dedicated to the promotion of a new feminism based on the teachings of Pope John Paul II. Sister Allen was previously a philosophy professor and department chair at St. John Vianney Seminary in Denver.*

to Noah. This first biblical record of intergenerational fruition records a history which will continue and make possible the Incarnation of Jesus Christ of the Virgin Mary in the fullness of time. This intergenerational fruition continues to the present day, as each one of us here is added to our own family's book of generations.

The deep reality of the spiritual dimension of marriage permeates Scripture from the beginning of Genesis through the prophet Hosea's description of the Lord's fidelity to the marriage covenant: "I will betroth you to me forever; I will betroth you to me in righteousness and in justice, in steadfast love, and in mercy. I will betroth you to me in faithfulness; and you shall know the Lord" (Hosea 2:19–20). This intergenerational fruition of marriage will continue until it is brought to completion in the heavenly marriage described in the Book of Revelation: "The Spirit and the bride say, 'Come.' Let him who is thirsty come, let him who desires take the water of life without price" (22:17).

Gender reality includes sex identity.

Much of what is revealed through faith can also be discovered in the world through human reason and observation of the senses. This is the work of scientists who identify the forms of real things. Scientists also explain the embedded relations of conjugate forms within an organic human being, e.g. of cells in an organ or an organ in a system. Organic nature often has some exceptions to laws about the forms of things. These exceptions do not destroy the rule or a law. Aristotle described science as concerned with "what is always or for the most part" true. Exceptions occur and remain in the lives of persons who may genuinely suffer from them, such as a person who may embody some ambiguity in sex identity or for a married woman and man who are unable to conceive a child. It often is a great suffering for a person to embody such an exception to the forms in nature. Yet the forms of what is always or is usually the case in scientific laws remain.

Philosophers integrate discoveries of the various sciences. Catholic philosophers also consider the relation of scientific discoveries to truths revealed by faith. Even though philosophy and science contain an admixture of truth and error, they are self-correcting over time. Since truth cannot contradict itself, eventually these complementary pathways of the human spirit to truth inch ever closer towards the one truth known to God and made available to us.

We are most fortunate to live in a time of history when many important truths revealed in Scripture about the integral complementarity of woman and man have been verified by science and philosophy. For example, when the authors of Genesis wrote the history of the book of generations and when Aristotle wrote his book *Generation of Animals,* nearly everyone thought that only the man provided fertile seed for generation. The contribution of ovulation by women took over two thousand years to be discovered and verified by science.

We know the truth about conception today. This truth confirms all four principles of complementarity at the level of sexually differentiated contribution to generation. Women and men provide a contribution of equal dignity to generation in the same number of chromosomes. They provide a significant difference in both the structure of one of the chromosomes and in the specific way a woman generates in herself and a man generates in another. When this way of relation occurs at the fertile time for conception, then their relation is often synergetic. When a human being is conceived and the mother fosters its growth through birth, then the real, integral complementarity of the woman and man becomes intergenerationally fruitful. This is gender reality.

A simple way to depict the difference between sex identity and gender identity is to say that our sex identity is (always or for the most part) male or female. It is a one-dimensional point of reference. An infant has a sex identity verified by science in chromosomes, anatomy, and physiology.

Our gender identity is a three-dimensional point of reference. Its starting point is our sexual embodiment as male or female. Gender identity also includes the other layers of human existence, namely, our consciousness, our self-awareness, our maturing self-development, self-mastery, self-governance, relations with others, and often our relation in prayer with the God who has created us for a specific vocation. We form ourselves over time individually into a particular way of being a man or of being a woman. An adult person has a gender identity, he or she acts in the world as a man or as a woman. These acts are respectively feminine in the case of a woman and masculine in the case of a man. So the three dimensions of gender are man-male-masculine or woman-female-feminine.

Gender reality is about the whole woman and the whole man. It is not just about sex activity. The married relation is a relation of integral gender complementarity and not just a fractional gender identity. The etymological root of gender, *gen,* means to reproduce, to breed, and to generate. Sex activity is tied to sex identity, and in marriage, the meaning of sex identity, as male or female, is embedded in the meaning of gender identity of a man or woman. Sex activity is not the whole of gender identity; nor is it an irrelevant part of gender identity. Gender reality includes sex identity whether or not there is sex activity. We all need to use the word 'gender' in its meaning of gender reality.

Unfortunately, in the history of philosophy, the lack of knowledge of a woman's equal contribution to generation with man led to a systematic, almost ideological, devaluation of woman's dignity for over two thousand years. The view of the male as naturally superior to the female permeated philosophical, scientific, and cultural attitudes. It harmed innocent women and girls in many hidden and other not-so-hidden ways. Many of those who supported it were blinded to contrary evidence. Many men preferred to be thought of as naturally superior to women. In the last hundred years a reversal has begun to occur. Many women today view themselves as naturally superior to men. This has led them to adopt an almost ideological devaluation of man's dignity. But today the truth about women and men is well known. There is no excuse left to defend anything other than the equal dignity and significant difference of women and men.

Sex and gender ideologies distort the truth about the relation of woman and man.

At the beginning of modern philosophy, Descartes reduced the human soul to a unisex rational mind and reduced the organic human body to inert matter. He also radically separated the mind from the body, effectively losing the point of integration within the human person.

In the last century two extremely destructive post-Cartesian ideologies emerged in the United States of America. They have now "gone viral" – to borrow a contemporary phrase – indicating their international dimensions. The first, sex ideology, arose in the works of Alfred Kinsey (1894–1956), an entomologist, one who studied insects. Kinsey reduced the human sexual act from an expression of genuine love between a woman and a man to a quantity of animal-like outlets. His research was filled with deceptive methods and publication of fabricated results. Like most ideologies, sex ideology harms the innocent.

The second destructive force was gender ideology, which first arose in the works of John Money (1921–2006), a psychologist. He considered gender to be a fluid mixture of many fragmented parts of a human being. He also thought that these parts could be reassembled in various combinations from birth to the age of two leading to five, ten, or fifteen so-called genders. Like Kinsey, Money used deceptive research methods and published distorted results, which were promoted on the unsuspecting public. He tried to turn a normal boy into a girl by surgery and other medical interventions. His experiment on this boy turned out to be a colossal, tragic failure. Money, however, continued to promote it as if it had been a great success. Before long, textbooks in the social sciences spread these erroneous views throughout the world.

When Kinsey's sex ideology merged with Money's gender ideology they became a lethal weapon against the human person, especially by portraying exceptions as the norm. The norm is that the human being is, always or for the most part, a male or a female and called into marriages and families. Many textbooks written by secular feminists continued to spread the virus of sex and gender ideology in wide-ranging academic, social, and political settings.

Fortunately, the self-correcting nature of scientific research has brought to light what was done in the dark by Kinsey and Money. Lawyers, journalists, and demographers like Mary Ann Glendon, Marguerite Peeters, Dale O'Leary, and Nicholas Eberstadt have carefully mapped the merged sex/gender ideologies. They have shown how the ideologists moved into world organizations like the United Nations and spread distortions about woman and man's identities around the world throughout unsuspecting countries. Paradoxically, feminist support for ultrasound examinations of pregnant women has resulted in the destruction of disproportionate numbers of baby girls. From my perspective the killing of even one unborn developing human being, male or female, is one too many.

Sex and gender ideologies have also harmed many adult women and men who have been caught in their grip. These ideologies distort the true equal dignity and significant difference of women and men; they ruin the gifts of synergetic relation and intergenerational fruition. Like a cancerous cell, these ideologies grow, often obliterating the true meaning of marriage in the minds of innocent boys and girls, women and men. Blessed Paul VI prophesied, in *Humanae Vitae* (n. 17), the harm that comes when a person reduces someone of the opposite gender to "a mere instrument for the satisfaction of his own desires." This reduction can reach the point where men and women begin to obliterate one another.

Complementarity flourishes on a true metaphysical foundation.

Gender ideology is built on a false metaphysical foundation which collapses into fragments of disconnected parts. Speaking as a philosopher, the false metaphysical foundation which describes persons as composites of multiple unconnected parts, or even of just two unconnected parts, as in a Platonic or Cartesian dualism, can never support what is known to be true about women and men and about marriage.

In contrast, gender reality is based on a true metaphysical foundation. Gender reality needs a descriptive metaphysics based on real beings in the world; it cannot be based on a revisionary metaphysics which tries to make the world conform to some idea invented by a human mind. A true descriptive metaphysics is found in a vitalized Thomism, which is flexible enough to incorporate advances in contemporary science.

By divine providence and the gift of the Holy Spirit, in the twentieth century when the false sex and gender ideologies of Kinsey and Money appeared on the world scene, several philosophers rose up to defend the human person and to provide insights into the integral complementarity of a woman and a man in marriage. Each one of these witnesses to the concept of complementarity experienced a religious awakening in an astounding gift of God to the world in its time of need.

Rescue came from Dietrich von Hildebrand's claim that a married woman and man are metaphysical complements. It also came from Emmanuel Mounier's personalist defense that a woman is also a person. It came from Jacques and Raïssa Maritain's interfaith Thomistic circles in Meudon. It came from Edith Stein (Saint Teresa Benedicta of the Cross) with her phenomenological elaboration of the engendered experience of being a woman or being a man. It came from Bernard Lonergan's integration of the conclusions of contemporary science into a revised metaphysics of hylomorphism, of the form/matter composite structure of real beings. And it came most of all from Pope Saint John Paul II's elaboration of the integral complementarity of a woman and a man on the physical, psychological, ontological, and spiritual levels. Saint John Paul II can truly be named "The Apostle of Integral Complementarity." He was the first to provide a completely integrated theory and opened up new depths and breadths in marriage, family, culture, and the vibrant communion of persons.

Flowing from Saint John Paul II's apostolic activity of teaching on the integral complementarity of a woman and a man in marriage, many other authors have gone forth to spread the good news. Some of them are present here today. I look forward to listening to the reflections of the men and women from the many different religious traditions present at this colloquium. Each one of you analogously bears witness to complementarity experienced and represented. Together, with the help of God, may we witness to the real truth, wonderful goodness, creative unity, and radiant beauty of the complementarity of a woman and a man in marriage!

"Buddhism talks about two orientations of love. . . . The love of bosatsu is not rooted in the ego. It is not until we start to pursue truth and justice as the objectives of our love, that our love becomes the love of bosatsu. . . . Love becomes eros when directed to the opposite sex; it becomes the love of bosatsu when directed to God and Buddha."

NISSHO TAKEUCHI

7

NISSHO TAKEUCHI

Toward a More Perfect Love

A Buddhist Perspective

IT CAN BE SAID that in today's society, tainted by modern civilization, few people correctly understand the meaning and the value of a legitimate marriage from the viewpoints of religious and philosophical-intellectual traditions. In this regard, I believe that this important communion between sexes must be examined in light of the universal principles of morals and ethics, as well as by the dignity of our religious values.

It is our fortune that the Congregation for the Doctrine of the Faith of the Holy See called on the world religions and provided an opportunity for learning about the ways of a good marriage as it ought to be. I would like to express my deep appreciation for this opportunity from the bottom of my heart. I am going to speak a few words from the viewpoint of Nichiren Shu, one of the traditional schools of Japanese Buddhism, based on the doctrines of our founder, Reverend Nichiren.

The ways of love between the sexes in marriage

When Buddhism talks about the ways of love between different sexes in the scope of marriage, it points out that there are two orientations of love, which require a strict distinction from each other. I'll speak first about the ways of love that Buddhism embraces.

Buddhism requires a man and a woman to deeply study the "teaching about love" based on the Buddhist doctrines, and in this process, to establish a solid confidence for realizing the ideal love of Shakyamuni Buddha in their own "self-personality."

Shakyamuni Buddha preaches that a marriage can cause hardship unless both parties, the man and the woman, work collaboratively as *shutai:* to turn themselves into an embodiment of the true love that is faithful to the Buddhist doctrines. (*Shutai* is based on relational thinking beyond subjectivity or objectivity. Working or acting as *shutai* refers to seeing issues that others are facing as your own, not seeing them as "other" but thinking in their shoes.) Those who embody the good love must be owners of the love vested in the ultimate *shogo* (doctrine to reach enlightenment) achieved by Shakyamuni Buddha, which is the love of *fuzen'nu* (uncorrupted by *bon'no*, the destructive emotions), the highest love held by *bosatsu* (bodhisattva).

✦ ABBOT NISSHO TAKEUCHI *is chair of the Sohjoh Nichiren School of Buddhism in Japan. He has been teaching corporate strategy and leadership to executives for over thirty years. He organized an International Peace Ceremony through Interreligious Cooperation and Dialogue annually from 1981 through 2011. Since 2012, he has been hosting the Citizens' Forum for Learning from Interreligious Dialogue.*

Love is inherently rooted in human emotions. However, it is not made of emotions only. It also involves our rational mind, which embraces the emotion of love, and our strong will, which supports our rational mind. We must understand all the related conditions and challenges as a comprehensive relatedness, and create an environment where both sexes mutually enable each other's characteristics and always communicate thoroughly with each other.

Now, the love in a marriage that Buddhist doctrines must not accept is the one that includes deep blindness and hypocrisy rooted in the human ego, which has a general tendency to focus heavily on appearance, to force the other to obey one's desire, and to seek sole ownership of the other, dominating over the other relentlessly.

If on any occasion either partner is one-sidedly denied or refused by the other, this love immediately triggers serious hatred between the two. The deeper the hypocritical love one has for the other, the deeper the hatred this love turns into. This is a typical disruption of the love of eros.

Just to note, besides the love between a man and a woman, or a married couple, which we discuss here, there are people who devote themselves to love of absolute purity. That is the love of parents and children, paternal and maternal love. Maternal love, in particular, the deep love given by mothers to their children continually and unconditionally without any self-interest, is nothing but a love of absolute purity.

However, even this pure love of mothers, the ultimate human love, still stands on the ego-personality that cannot go beyond the human boundary and is different from the love of *bosatsu*.

The essential difference between love of bombu and love of bosatsu

Now, I am going to speak about the difference between the love of *bombu* (an unenlightened person) and the love of *bosatsu*. First of all, every love that we generally experience as human beings, ranging from the love between a man and a woman to maternal and paternal love, is love that does not seek rewards for itself.

Nevertheless, this love is rooted in the ego-personality, which is love of eros. Even the mother's love, a love of thorough devotion which does not expect any rewards, stands on the ego-personality. This is because even the love that expects no return is still rooted in the ego that seeks fulfilment from its infinite devotion. A love of this kind is still the love of *bombu*.

Whether it is grasping love, by which a man and a woman try to gain an exclusive ownership of each other, or the so-called pure love of infinite devotion, it is the love of *bombu*. The act of taking fulfils one's ego, whereas the act of devoting fulfils one's self. Either way, ego and self are deeply interconnected at the bottom of our awareness.

A mother provides her selfless affection without asking for anything because the object is her own children. Her selfless affection is not given to other children. This means that in love of *bombu* there always exists an ego that incorporates a natural, instinctive function to seek realization of love by taking actions to be rewarded.

In contrast, the love of *bosatsu* is not rooted in the ego. It is not until we start to pursue truth and justice as the objectives of our love that our love becomes the love of *bosatsu* established in our self-personality.

Moreover, the love of *bosatsu* is not oriented to any particular objectives. In Buddhist doctrines, orienting one's love toward particular objectives is considered an ultimate *meimo* (confusion due to lack of enlightenment). The love of *bosatsu* is the way of love rooted in the self-personality that exists in the inner world of each and every human being.

However, in reality, a large majority of human beings always follow the emotional and exclusive love of *bombu* for others, which is based on the eros-centred ego personality. Is there any way to save us, who hold the love of *bombu* as our *bon'no*? What are the ways to *kaiken-sosei* (reveal and revive) the love of *bombu*? We ask this because, with these ways, we human beings can be saved.

Here, a Buddhist teaching says, the *myogi* (supreme doctrine) of *bon'no-soku-bodai* (earthly desires are nothing but enlightenment) can direct human beings to the right paths. In other words, it teaches us that faith means to seek God and Buddha with the same mind as we have for every love rooted in the ego. Just as one admires his parents, cares about children, and loves one's partner, one should seek the way to reach the wisdom of God and Buddha, which enables *bon'no* immediately to achieve *bodai* (enlightenment).

Love becomes eros when directed to the opposite sex; it becomes the love of *bosatsu* when directed to God and Buddha. Therefore, it is not that there are two kinds of love. Although the essence of love is one, there are two paths regarding the orientation of our love.

If a man and a woman, who presuppose a marriage, truly understand the meanings and the values of love of *bombu* and love of *bosatsu* and successfully establish this love of *bosatsu* in their self-personality, they will be able to lead a contented marriage throughout their lifetime. It is because the couple firmly believes that they will stay with God and Buddha residing in each other's inner world, through which they can wholeheartedly accept the presence of the other within their self-personality at the same time.

The integrated inner world of the self and the other

We must realize the fact that it is the way we perceive ourselves that overwhelmingly determines the impressions we receive from those around us. Our love of others and, conversely, our hatred for others almost perfectly reflect our own love and hatred towards the positive and negative images of ourselves within us.

Generally we are fond of others who are similar to our preferable images of ourselves inside us, and in fact we feel almost mysteriously strong attractions to them. In contrast, we cannot help having a clear emotion of hatred, to ourselves to a surprising extent, when we see others with the same unpleasant characteristics that we have within us.

When we meet with others, we are not seeing them as themselves. We are seeing ourselves through them. Through the others we encounter, we are being awakened to all the realities that are hidden inside our self, our self-personality including every possibility sealed within it.

In conclusion, the wonderful spiritual intelligence and moral personality that you find in others reflect the highest world of spiritual intelligence and moral personality to shape your own self, and that you are already hoping to cherish. The delightful relatedness of a married couple becomes promised when, through loving the other, you successfully discover the world of the highest self-personality that had been hidden inside you.

"Saint Paul's analogy between the husband-wife relationship and the rapport of Christ with the church sheds light on the divine mystery . . ."

JEAN LAFFITTE

8

JEAN LAFFITTE

The Sacramental Reality of Human Love

A Catholic Perspective

DEAR FRIENDS, it is my distinct honor and personal pleasure to share with you a perspective on what the Catholic Church considers as her and the whole of humanity's treasure: namely, human love seen in the context of creation and the intention of the Creator.

I have been asked to do it from the extraordinary contribution of Saint John Paul II, recently called the "Pope of the Family" by our present Holy Father, Pope Francis. Philosopher, theologian, moralist , pastor, Karol Wojtyła first, John Paul II later, was extremely committed to articulating and transmitting an authentic Christian anthropology founded upon what he called God's design on marriage and family, *consilium Dei matrimonii ac familiae.*

My task in this presentation will be to speak specifically about the sacramentality of human love.

It seems that conjugal love has ceased to be good news to the eyes of some of our contemporaries, who rather identify themselves more with the Pharisees interrogating Jesus in the Gospel of Matthew, chapter 19. The Pharisees asked Jesus a trick question on the Mosaic Law concerning the repudiation of one's wife through the bill of divorce. Jesus, instead, brought their attention to the initial order of creation:

> "Haven't you read," he replied, "that at the beginning the Creator made them male and female, and said: For this reason a man will leave his father and mother and be united to his wife, and the two will become one flesh? So they are no longer two, but one flesh. Therefore what God has joined together, let no one separate." (Matt. 19:4–6)

In the beginning, according to a definite plan, God created the world and formed the human person as male and female. Interpreting this plan, through and with the creation of Adam and Eve, Saint John Paul II teaches that humanity is to be constituted according to its sexual complementarity. But everything is done in the perspective of a divine plan; in this way, we see the unity between what Jesus wants and realizes (this is the theological

---

✦ BISHOP JEAN LAFFITTE, *secretary of the Pontifical Council for the Family, is a member of the Emmanuel Community and was ordained a priest in 1989. From 1990 to 1994, he was superior of the chaplains of Paray-le-Monial. He has taught ethics and the spirituality of marriage and family at the Pontifical John Paul II Institute and is the author of numerous publications, including most recently* La scelta della famiglia *(translated into several languages) and* Le Christ destin de l'homme.

aspect) and that which we are in reality (the anthropological aspect).

Even if there is a need to deepen the natural dimension of marriage, the church is called above all to carry out a mission that is specifically by nature theological, relative to salvation. The mission of the church is realized according to a modality that is sacramental, which is the most adequate way to express and transmit the truth of salvation. The sacrament of marriage actualizes, as do all the other sacraments, the baptismal immersion into the life, passion, death, and resurrection of Jesus Christ; marriage possesses all the riches and supernatural fruitfulness of a sacrament of salvation.

Marriage has a particular function that allows us to consider its proper mission: expressing in a particular way the nuptial mystery of Christ, the bridegroom, and of the church, his bride. It is inherent in the nature of the communion of life and love between man and woman to signify and actualize the union of Christ and the church. How is this possible? To understand this, we have to go back to the meaning of this primordial mystery and union between Christ and his church. This union is likewise characterized as communion of life and love: since it includes the divine good transmitted by Christ, it is a communication of eternal life and eternal love.

The mystery

Saint Paul in his letter to the Ephesians writes:

> Husbands, love your wives, just as Christ loved the church and gave himself up for her, in order to make her holy by cleansing her with the washing of water by the word, so as to present the church to himself in splendor,

> without a spot or wrinkle or anything of the kind – yes, so that she may be holy and without blemish. In the same way, husbands should love their wives as they do their own bodies. He who loves his wife loves himself. For no one ever hates his own body, but he nourishes and tenderly cares for it, just as Christ does for the church, because we are members of his body. "For this reason a man will leave his father and mother and be joined to his wife, and the two will become one flesh." This is a great mystery, and I am applying it to Christ and the church. (Eph. 5:22–33).

For Saint Paul, human love is not understood and explained on the basis of its definition or content, but from the perspective of the divine purpose. Thus, it reveals and unfolds itself over time. The divine mystery accomplishes, realizes, and consumes itself in the love of Jesus Christ, crucified and risen. What is the connection between the original love of man and woman and Jesus' sacrificial love? Each of these corresponds with the Creator's loving plan; but the former was wounded and bears in itself the traces of sin. Marriage, as an expression of love, not only continues having the prophetic power of proclaiming the love of God the Creator, but it also becomes a new reality, renewed by the love of Christ, who gives himself to his own, to his church, and unites himself with her, like a husband with his wife. Marriage becomes a sacrament of the redeeming love of Christ and expresses it effectively.

Saint John Paul II, in his first catechesis on human love, spoke of marriage as an expression of the Creator's love and, in this sense and only in this derivative sense, called it the primordial sacrament. More frequently, in the years that followed the publication of these extraordinary teachings, he continued referring to "God's plan for marriage and the family" to designate the original love between a man and a woman. In contrast, the term "mystery" is used in the Pauline sense of the redemptive union between Christ and the church.

Logically, the place of marriage within the realization of God's love in the person of Jesus Christ, who died and rose, gives marriage a specifically ecclesial dimension: if the church is the communication of divine love to humankind, accomplished through and in Christ, how could marriage express this love outside the church? The love between man and woman is great precisely in the light of this divine mystery. Saying this doesn't discredit the natural value of this reality, which is deeply written in the very being of man and woman. On the contrary, it implies seeing in it an implicit reference with the union of Christ and his church.

The meaning of marriage is accomplished in Christ, though it essentially keeps its original significance. Willed by God, it is the expression of the Creator's initial goodness: "Marriage, as a primordial sacrament, is assumed and inserted into the integral structure of the new sacramental economy, arising from redemption in the form, I would say, of a prototype. . . . All the sacraments of the new covenant find their prototype in marriage as the primordial sacrament."[1]

BEFORE GOING into the details of what Saint Paul's text teaches about our subject, we need to take a look at the broader context into which it is placed. We know that the Letter to the Ephesians begins with a presentation of God's eternal plan to make all people his children through Jesus Christ. Christ is placed above all things and appointed as head of the church, which is his body. Christ's mystery is where God reveals himself, but it is in the church that he makes himself known and accessible to humanity. The relationship between Christ and the church is analogous to the rapport between the head and the body: Christ is head of his body, which is the church. We have the first analogy: the head-body relationship, which is developed in the first chapters of Ephesians. This is followed by different instructions, among which we will mention only the one that interests us here: that of loving as Christ did, proposed by the Apostle as the model: "Therefore, be imitators of God, as beloved children, and live in love, as Christ loved us and gave himself up for us, a fragrant offering and sacrifice to God" (Eph. 5:1–2).

After this, some instructions that constitute domestic morality are given; these involve not only the relationship between the spouses – the main object of our attention – but also the relationship between the other members of the family community (chapter 6 and following). Let us therefore retain the essential point: the example to imitate is Christ's love, manifested by the total gift of himself, a gift that, because of our sin, has a sacrificial and redemptive form.

The connection between the body and the sacrament

Every sacrament supposes a physical reality. It is in fact the sign of something; it refers to another reality. Obviously, in order to be meaningful, a sign has to be visible. This is a requirement related to the condition of the Incarnation. The reality to be signified is, in view of Ephesians,

Christ's love. Since this is a spiritual reality, it has to be signified by a visible sign.

The visible sign of Christ's love is his dead and risen body. The fact that this body is risen indicates that it is also a sacrament of the Father's love, because the Son offered himself in sacrifice to the Father, who had the power to deliver him from death.

The Pauline example of Christ's love is presented especially to spouses: "Husbands should love their wives as their own bodies. . . . Since Christ did this for his own body, a man should leave his father and mother and be joined to his wife . . ." In these passages, the word "body" is used with two different meanings: in the literal sense, it refers to the body of the man or the woman, a corporeal reality that allows them to unite and become one flesh; and in an analogical sense, the church is called the Body of Christ, and this suggests the depth and intensity of the relationship of God's Son to his people. This bond expresses the realization, in Christ, of the mystery we have already mentioned, and which fully occupies the intention of the Letter to the Ephesians.

The sexual union between man and woman is understood as a reciprocal gift that each one offers to the other; the human body is considered with its sexual differentiation: masculinity and femininity. This fact is essential, although it does go against certain trends in our contemporary culture, which do not consider sexual complementarity as a fundamental anthropological structure. On this point, how can we not remember the talented way in which one of Saint John Paul II's catecheses related this basic fact to the theme of the image of God:

> Man becomes the image of God not so much in the moment of solitude as in the moment of communion. Right from the beginning, he is not only an image in which the solitude of a person who rules the world is reflected, but also, and essentially, an image of an inscrutable divine communion of persons.[2]

Paul's analogy between the husband-wife relationship and the rapport of Christ with the church sheds light on the divine mystery; in other words, it tells us something about the mutual love between Christ and the church. Yet, at the same time, it teaches about the essential truth of marriage, the purpose of which is to reflect Christ's gift to the church and her reciprocating love.

This reflection is not merely a likeness produced by simple imitation of the loving Christ; it is rather an indication of the presence – albeit partial – of the same mystery in the heart of conjugal love. Here, we need both Pauline analogies. We have already discussed the first one: the analogy of the head and the body. What does it correspond to in married life? Insofar as it emphasizes an organic bond between Christ and the church, it has an ecclesiological meaning: the church is the body that lives thanks to Christ. The analogy refers to a somatic unity of the human organism. Applied to a man and a woman, the image signifies the organic union they form, the *una caro* (one flesh) that they constitute. The second analogy is that of the husband-wife relationship. Christ wanted to make his bride holy by cleansing her with the water of baptism and the word of life that expresses nuptial love: the water-bath is an immediate preparation of the bride (that is the church) for Christ the bridegroom. Baptism, in this sense, makes the Christian partake in Christ's spousal love.

Another verse: the bridegroom presents the church to himself in splendor, without spot or wrinkle . . . but holy and without blemish (v. 25) symbolically indicates the moment of the wedding, that is when the bride, dressed in the wedding gown, is led to the husband. In this expression we can also see an eschatological dimension: at the end of time, the Bride will be eternally united with her Bridegroom, and she will be without spot or wrinkle, but instead holy and without blemish.

Mystery and sacrament

"This is a great mystery, and I mean in reference to Christ and the church" (Eph. 5:32). The marriage of Christ and the church takes place on the cross, where the fruitfulness of the Holy Spirit is given. If the sacrament intends to express the great mystery – as Saint Paul says – we must admit that it cannot ever do this perfectly. The mystery always exceeds the sacrament, not because of some kind of insufficiency of the sacrament, but because of human limitations: the sacrament reveals the mystery, but it implies the assent of faith. However, as Saint John Paul II pointed out in his catechesis on September 8, 1982, it is something more than the simple meaning or the mere proclamation of the mystery: it is able also to realize it in us.

The sacramental union of man and woman accomplishes in each spouse the mystery of divine love, hidden for ages and revealed by Christ's sacrifice on the cross. The love between man and woman is inscribed in the logic of salvation that reaches beyond us, but gradually reveals itself; through the sacramental sign of marriage, this love becomes able not only to signify this salvation but also to implement all of its efficiency.

Baptism definitively introduces man and woman into the new and eternal covenant, into the nuptial covenant of Christ and the church. Precisely because of this indestructible insertion, the intimate communion of life and love, founded by the Creator, is elevated and brought into the spousal charity of Christ, sustained and enriched by his redeeming power. With this being said, allow me now to move to the subject of the presence of the mystery of Christ the bridegroom in the Eucharistic gift he makes of himself to his church.

The sacrificial and spousal dimension of the Eucharist gift

The institution of the Eucharist responds, in Luke and John, to Jesus' burning desire to celebrate the Passover with his disciples. Beyond the usual ritual – the banquet of the feast, in which the master of the banquet (usually the father) blesses the cup of thanksgiving and breaks the bread – the disciples share a moment of intense communion that Jesus' words make especially significant: "This is my body given for you; this cup is the new covenant in my blood, which is poured out for you" (Luke 22:19-20). These words anticipate Jesus' free gift of himself, the divine love, which inspires the nature of a sacrifice. The Last Supper leads Jesus into his Passion: "Jesus did not simply state," wrote Saint John Paul II, "that what he was giving them to eat and drink was his body and his blood; he also expressed its sacrificial meaning and made sacramentally present his sacrifice which would soon be offered on the cross for the salvation of all" (*Ecclesia de*

Eucharistia, n. 12). The life offered is also signified by the gesture of offering separately the bread and the wine: the body is given first so that the blood that flows from it, the blood that is poured out, may mean the actual gift of life. This sacrifice is an act of supreme love: "He loved them to the end" (John 13:1).

The body that is given and the blood that is shed not only have a symbolic value: they are offered as food and drink to the disciples who, intentionally assembled with Jesus and with each other, and are now sacramentally – that is, really – united to him. Jesus' paschal gift on the cross, thus entrusted to his church, constituted at that moment and one flesh with Christ: "the Eucharistic *una caro* – one body – sealed in the blood of the cross and offered to all generations in the Eucharistic celebration, thus brings the nuptial mystery of Christ and the church to its full completion."[3] This is very concrete: being really united to Christ means partaking in his redemptive sacrifice. The disciples who receive the body and blood of Christ become co-corporeal (Eph. 3:6) with him (and consanguineous, if we may say so). We understand why union of charity is the requisite for receiving, with dignity and efficiency, the body and blood of Christ: this gift of divine love is given to the entire church, the bride of Christ, and continuously regenerates her. The essence of the Eucharist is thus spousal: it is the gift the bridegroom gives to his bride and that the bride receives with faith.

The redemption of human love, or the purification of the gift

The event on Calvary and Christ's resurrection determine the whole sacramental economy, present and transmitted in all the sacraments. Marriage is in a special way – in Saint Paul's perspective – connected to the mystery of redemption, and this has made it, in this sense, a prototype, as John Paul II put it, of all other sacramental signs. We now understand this better: as primordial sacrament, it is the model according to which salvation is accomplished, the spousal gift received by the church-bride. "The original unity resides in the fact," Balthasar writes, "that the church was fashioned out of Christ just as Eve was fashioned out of Adam: She flowed from the pierced side of the Lord as he slept on the cross. She . . . is his body, just as Eve was the flesh of Adam's flesh."[4]

The new sacramental action is not offered to Adam and Eve before the fall, but to those who bear the weight of original sin, and in whom the flesh desires what is opposed to the Spirit, and the Spirit desires what is opposed to the flesh (Gal. 5:17). The drama of sin prevents the donation from bearing fruit with the magnitude and the strength present in the Creator's original plan. The gift that characterizes the covenant of the spouses needs to be continually purified: the ethos of the gift is an ethos of redemption, to use the words of Saint John Paul II's catecheses (19, 49). Here, the word "ethos" signifies the free accomplishment by the spouses of the truth inscribed in their being.

To be precise, redemption leads to the consolidation of all the aspects of this natural truth; thus, for example, it strengthens the indissoluble character of the covenant between the spouses, which existed when creation began (the principle Jesus indicates to the Pharisees, but that their hard-heartedness prevented them from perceiving, in Matthew 19). The body of the spouses, sacramentally inscribed in the horizon of redemption, experiences the assumption of all the original values inscribed in its nature. This excludes, for example, adultery, which not only contradicts the nature of the marital covenant, but also deprives the body of its deeper meaning (adultery will never be a gift); adultery – the fact is better understood in this light – is incompatible with the reception of the body and blood of Christ; but redemption is also operating, primarily within man, purifying his heart, because it is in the heart that evil desires are born: "I say to you that everyone who looks at a woman with lust has already committed adultery with her in his heart" (Matt. 5:27–28). In an indirect interpretation of the text, Saint John Paul II has extraordinarily strong words: "Jesus assigns as a duty to every man the dignity of every woman: and simultaneously (even though only in an indirect way) to every woman the dignity of every human."[5]

The redemption of the body establishes the spouses in the hope of the revelation of the children of God (Rom. 8:19), when the love of charity that inspired the life of the husband and the wife in the transient condition of the world will continue. The very form of the sacrament of marriage, the words of consent exchanged by the spouses, "I take you for my wife, for my husband," imply "precisely that perennial, unique, and unrepeatable language of the body," as noted in Saint John Paul II's catechesis (18). The term "language of the body" points to the interpretation which man and woman can grasp as inscribed in their nature (sexual nature), which enables them to signify in their bodies the mutual gift of themselves which they are offering to one another, through the exercise of the sexual faculties. The redemption of the body anticipates the time of the resurrection, because only after their resurrection will man and woman be fully given to the truth that embraces the totality of what they are (and in particular the truth of their corporal nature). Here, as baptized, it is in Christ that spouses are given to each other.

So, the spouses take part in the sacrificial life of Christ, because the spouses publicly manifest their membership in the church by a gift that unites them in Christ. This gift belongs to the church. Their participation in the nuptial mystery of Christ and the church is an objective and permanent fact. It is public and therefore visible, and hence the reality of their life becomes an efficacious sign of the mystery of Christ's love for his church.

In the post-synodal exhortation *Familiaris Consortio,* Saint John Paul II states:

> The content of participation in Christ's life is also specific: conjugal love involves a totality, in which all the elements of the person enter – appeal of the body and instinct, power of feeling and affectivity, aspiration of the spirit and of will. It aims at a deeply personal unity, the unity that, beyond union in one flesh, leads to forming one heart and soul. (n. 13)

The configuration of the spouses to Christ, often called their consecration, is in no way an outward imitation or a remote analogy: it is the work of the Holy Spirit, who deeply transforms the spouses' subjectivity and their ability to love as Christ loved us. It sanctifies their love for one another by purifying it, so that this love becomes that of Christ himself in ecclesial witness, accomplished day after day.

Indeed, the whole question of the indissolubility of Christian marriage could be formulated on the basis of what it is in truth called to express: love without reticence, which is Christ's gift to all people. This fact is just as unique as the gift a man or a woman makes of himself or herself in sacramental marriage.

1. John Paul II, "Marriage an Integral Part of New Sacramental Economy," General Audience of Wednesday, 20 October 1982, in *L'Osservatore Romano Weekly Edition in English,* 25 October 1982, p. 2.
2. John Paul II, "Man Becomes the Image of God by Communion of Persons," General Audience of Wednesday, 14 November 1979, in *L'Osservatore Romano Weekly Edition in English,* 19 November 1979, p. 1.
3. M. Ouellet, "Il sacramento del Matrimonio e il mistero nuziale di Cristo," in Renzo Bonetti, *Eucarestia e matriminio: unico mistero nuziale* (Rome: Città Nuova, 2000).
4. H. U. von Balthasar, *Christlicher Lebensstand* (Ital.: *Gli Stati di vita del Cristiano,* 202–203).
5. John Paul II, "Christ Opened Marriage to the Saving Action of God," General Audience of 24 November 1982, in *L'Osservatore Romano Weekly Edition in English,* 29 November 1982, p. 9.

"The biblical picture of man and woman together in marriage is not something about which we can say, 'Oh well, they had some funny ideas back then. We know better now.' The biblical view of marriage is part of the larger whole of new creation, and it symbolizes and points to that divine plan."

N. T. WRIGHT

9

N. T. WRIGHT

From Genesis to Revelation

An Anglican Perspective

I'VE BEEN ASKED to talk to you today about the big biblical picture within which we bring into focus the whole question of the complementary of man and woman, particularly of course in marriage.

One of the fascinating things about the Bible as we now have it – as you know, it was written over rather a long period of time – is that it begins and ends with the coming together of heaven and earth. Right at the beginning of the book of Genesis, we have those two complementary accounts of creation (Genesis chapter 1 and chapter 2, broadly speaking), and from the beginning we are told that God made heaven and earth; and that, so it seems, heaven and earth are supposed to work together. We in the Western world have often thought of heaven and earth as radically separate, as completely distinct. Indeed, some people have constructed whole philosophies in which heaven is so far away that it seems as though it has nothing whatever to do with earth. But in Genesis it's not like that. Heaven and earth are supposed to be the twin interlocking spheres of God's good creation.

Then, as the story in Genesis 1 unfolds, we discover that there are all sorts of other things in God's creation which mirror that, which reflect it, which are likewise supposed to be complementaries. So we have not only heaven and earth; we have the sea and the dry land, we have plants and animals – a different sort of differentiation, but a differentiation nonetheless. Then, within the animal kingdom, we have of course male and female, and indeed also within the plant kingdom up to a point. And then the story reaches its great climax with the creation of human beings in the image of God: male and female together.

When we read and re-read this extraordinary account in Genesis 1 – and it is one of the most remarkable pieces of writing from the whole ancient world – then we see that these complementaries all reinforce one another and are meant to work together, so that the man and the woman together are a symbol of something which is profoundly true of creation as a whole. Not that the man represents heaven and the woman represents earth; that's

---

✦ RT. REV. NICHOLAS THOMAS WRIGHT *is professor of New Testament and Early Christianity at the University of St. Andrews in Scotland. Wright was bishop of Durham in the Church of England from 2003 until his retirement in 2010. Among his many writings are his* Christian Origins and the Question of God *series and the* For Everyone *series, a commentary on the New Testament, completed in 2011. Wright received DPhil and DD degrees from Oxford and taught New Testament studies for twenty years at Cambridge, McGill, and Oxford Universities.*

a mistake that was made in some ancient paganism. The point, rather, is that the idea of these two being designed to go together, to work together, is a very profound reality at the heart of that whole story of God's good creation.

Then in Genesis 2 the focus changes and we have a different kind of story, but one which nonetheless also converges on the idea of man and woman coming together, now more explicitly in marriage: one leaves one's parents and cleaves to one's spouse, so that the two become one flesh (2:24). These two creation stories, which of course are not meant to be photographic reproductions of "what happened at the beginning," are themselves great symbolic pointers – signposts towards a deeper, stranger reality which human words are probably unable to express. That's how symbols, including biblical symbols, work. And so, right there at the start of the whole Bible as we have it and at the start of the book of Genesis, we have this rich symbolic account of God's good creation in which, at its very heart, the coming together of male plus female is itself a signpost pointing to that great complementarity of God's whole creation, of heaven and earth belonging together.

When we then jump in a huge sweep to the very end of the Bible – and again, historically speaking, it's some kind of a providential accident that the book of Revelation is now at the end of the Christian canon of scripture – we find in Revelation 21 and 22 substantially the same thing, only now at the end of the story rather than at the point of its beginning. Indeed, whoever wrote the book of Revelation – Saint John the Divine as he is traditionally called – I think must have known, as he wrote those last two amazing chapters, that this was how the story which began in Genesis was designed to reach its proper conclusion. In his vision, the new Jerusalem is coming down from heaven like a bride adorned for her husband. This symbolism of marriage, of male and female coming together (only now it is the church which is the new Jerusalem, coming together with Christ as the bridegroom), tells us that here we find the very heart of God's intended creation. Heaven and earth were always meant for one another, and now at last that's what's going to happen.

Of course, in the Western tradition particularly, we Christians have often thought the name of the game was to leave earth and go to heaven instead, but that's simply a parody. To be sure, there is much about earth as it is at the moment which is sad, dark, gloomy, and evil. We want to be rid of all that, and to be with God instead. But the whole point of the biblical revelation is that the God who made heaven and earth together in the first place is going to renew them, so that the end of the whole story will not be "heaven" by itself, but God's new heaven and new earth. We shouldn't be surprised, then, that the symbol for that reality is again marriage, the coming together of the man and the woman, in this case, of Jesus Christ and of his church, as the sign and pointer that this is what God had in mind all along.

Now it's important to begin with that big picture. If we don't, we can easily imagine that what the Bible has to say about men and women, about marriage, about all that follows from and surrounds that complicated and rich and exciting topic, is simply a set of rules. We in the Western church have tended to isolate rules from the rest of the picture. We have imagined that the purpose

God wants for us is to leave "earth" behind and to go to "heaven" instead, and that God has in the meantime given us these somewhat arbitrary regulations for how he wants us to behave. (Sometimes people say that if we keep the rules we'll get to heaven; sometimes people say that those who are going to heaven for a different reason, because they believe the gospel, should still keep the rules because that's what God wants; but in either case there is no organic link between the rules and the ultimate goal.) So people then begin to say, "Well, these 'rules' might have been different; we know much better now than people did a long time ago; anyway perhaps the rules were just made up by human teachers who wanted to stop people enjoying themselves . . ." and so on.

Now that isn't just a parody of the truth. It is actually a radical distortion of what the Bible is all about. As humans we are called to live as symbols of the heaven-and-earth creation which was given at the beginning and which is to be consummated, as in the book of Revelation, at the end. There are many other passages, in the Bible as a whole and particularly the New Testament, which speak in this rich symbolic way of the purpose of God. Let me give just one or two examples.

At the end of the great chapter we call Romans 8, one of the most extraordinary passages in the whole of the New Testament, we find Paul expounding with delight and almost glee the sense that the whole creation is on tip-toe with expectation because it is going to be set free from its bondage of decay to share the liberty of the glory of the children of God. He is there using the imagery of "new birth," of the new creation being born from the womb of the old. This is a fertile image, a female, birth-giving image. He is treating the picture of a woman giving birth as a signpost, a pointer, to the fact that this is what the whole creation was made for. That reinforces the picture that, from Genesis to Revelation, we have a framework, biblical "bookends" if you like, and when we move in towards the rest of the Bible we see how many other things there mean what they mean within that larger context and framework.

Obviously a lot of the Old Testament is concerned with the special relationship between God and his people Israel, the people of the family of Abraham. From the very beginning, that is spoken of and imaged in terms of a marriage, a covenant, a partnership: God is like the bridegroom, Israel is like the bride. That corresponds to the very beginning: with Adam and Eve in the garden, there is a purpose. It isn't just that God and Israel are to be there together, while the rest of creation can do what it likes. When God and Israel get together, this covenant has a purpose, and its purpose is new creation. The whole of the biblical revelation consists of that movement from creation to new creation, from covenant to new covenant. The covenant between God and Israel (and then between Christ and the church, which we'll come to in a moment), points to, effects, and symbolizes that renewal of all creation.

We shouldn't be surprised, then, that the New Testament writers pick up that idea of God and Israel and transpose it, translate it, into the language of Christ and the church. This comes out particularly clearly in Paul's letter to the Ephesians, where in chapter 5 he puts together the advice and counsel to husbands and wives with one of the most stunning and striking pictures of the relationship between Jesus and the people whom he has redeemed. Jesus gives his life for his people; his people respond in gratitude and love. The vocation of husbands and wives is not absolutely identical with this, but it is modeled on it. It symbolizes and points on to the deeper and richer relationship between Christ and the church. (That takes us back once more to Revelation chapters 21 and 22.)

In Ephesians, the framework that Paul himself constructs for this teaching includes the telling and crucial introductory comment in chapter 1, that the entire divine purpose always was to sum up all things in heaven and on earth in the Messiah. Then in chapter 2 this is symbolized in the coming together of Jew and Gentile into the one Spirit-filled family; indeed, in chapter 3 Paul speaks of the church as a family with God as its father, before working that out in terms of the unity and holiness of the church in chapters 4 and 5. What he says about husbands and wives in chapter 5 therefore comes within a larger context where in and through Jesus Christ the whole world is brought into a new unity.

That is the larger framework within which we can understand the detailed teaching of the Bible about marriage itself. Here is a point which people often find strange. Frequently folk imagine that the way the Bible works goes like this: the Old Testament is full of rules and regulations, and then the New Testament says "don't worry about those old rules – we don't believe in law any more. We just live by grace." That again is a complete caricature of the way the Bible works. What you actually find in the scriptures is that from the beginning, God's people have an impetus towards the coming together of one man and one woman in marriage. But Abraham has more than one wife. Isaac is one of the very few patriarchs who, so far as we can tell, have only one. Jacob has two, and then two concubines as well. And by the time we get to David and Solomon we have ancient Near Eastern polygamy in full swing. The biblical writers don't seem too bothered about that. Of course, David's adultery is a big problem. And when Solomon takes more foreign wives, that's a problem too, particularly because they divert his heart from single-minded devotion to the one true God. But though the Old Testament does reiterate the ideal of one man and one woman, this is not a major theme, and some of the great biblical heroes seem to flout it completely.

But when we get to the New Testament, we find something which goes clean against the assumption I mentioned a moment ago. We might expect, based on the received assumption, that we would move from a strict moral demand in the Old Testament to a slackening of moral tension in the New. Not a bit of it. Jesus is very clear, in Mark 10 and elsewhere: now that he is there, launching God's kingdom, renewing the covenant between God and his people, the creation itself is being renewed. He goes back to the beginning, to Genesis 1 and 2: God made them male and female, and insisted that the two would become one.

This was, to say the least, unexpected. Jesus' first followers were puzzled, as many are today, by the clear and strict simplicity of what he says. His own disciples asked him how it would work out, and Jesus explained that from the beginning this was how God planned it. He grants that, in Deuteronomy, Moses gave permission for divorce. But this, he says, was because of "the hardness of your hearts" (Mark 10:5).

This is one of many places in the gospel story where it seems that Jesus is hinting or implying that what is on offer in his message is a cure for the hardness of human hearts. That is a huge challenge, as much today as it was in Jesus' day. It takes a lot of pastoral working out. These are difficult and dark areas where many people struggle today, as they have always done.

But that is the picture, and that's why it means what it means. It isn't that Jesus is saying, "Here is an absolute demand, and if you can't make it then God can't love you." He is saying, "Here is the way humans were meant to be, and if you follow me we'll make it a reality." Actually, humans know in their bones that this is how we were meant to be. And what we all half-know (though we become skilled at covering up this knowledge), God gives in the new creation of the Gospel. In this area, as in all others, we cannot achieve it in our own strength. We are invited to take it as a gift.

As we do so, and then follow that through the teaching about man and woman which we find in the rest of the New Testament, we discover again and again that it isn't just an odd rule, a rule which we might in our day object to on the basis that we have new and different scientific knowledge about how human beings actually are. It is always a statement of faith about the meaning of God's creation and about God's ultimate purposes for that creation.

Of course in our day we have had the prevailing mood of modern Western secularism. This goes back to a long tradition first of Deism, and then actually to a modern version of ancient Epicureanism. This gives people the idea that if there is a heaven, if there is a God, they are so far away as to be for all practical purposes irrelevant, so we might as well treat them as non-existent. So people in the Western world have lived with an implicit worldview which says, "Religion is about escaping earth and getting to heaven." Then the "realists," who think of themselves as having their feet firmly on the earth, don't want to have anything to do with heaven or God at all.

We have inhaled the air of philosophies like that for so long that we shouldn't be surprised to find ourselves, in our cultures and our societies, symbolizing something of the same in our human relationships. Split heaven and earth apart and you will split other things apart as well, one of them being marriage. That is one of many reasons why, today, many people both inside and outside the church find the biblical norm – the new-creation, new-covenant ideal of husband and wife – so hard to maintain. It is indeed something many of us have to work hard at. It's tough being a Christian in today's world. It's tough being a husband or a wife; it's tough making family life work. But that is because it is a sign and a symbol of the most extraordinary divine plan, the plan which cost God himself the death of his own beloved son. That is how God brought heaven and earth together: the death and resurrection of Jesus, nothing less. And that has to be worked out in every area of Christian faithfulness.

This shouldn't surprise us. Jesus himself, and every great teacher of the faith, made it clear. To follow him means taking up the cross. It costs us the equivalent of the cross, in the moral struggle through which we fulfill our calling in baptism: to die daily, to be generous, to be wise, to be humble, to be forgiving, to be patient, to be loving; to be, in other words, whole human beings. Marriage,

the coming together of one man and one woman, is the context within which so much of that is symbolized and actualized.

That is why, I believe, the biblical picture of man and woman together in marriage is not something about which we can say, "Oh well, they had some funny ideas back then. We know better now." The biblical view of marriage is part of the larger whole of new creation, and it symbolizes and points to that divine plan. Every time I, as a priest, celebrate the marriage of a couple, I remind myself, and I frequently remind the couple, that what we are doing is setting up a signpost. We live in a world of many storms and many winds; those signposts can easily get battered and broken. But they are pointing somewhere; and the reality to which they are pointing is the fulfillment of God's good purposes for creation. Marriage is a sign of all things in heaven and on earth coming together in Christ. That's why it is a tough calling. But that is why, also, it is central and non-negotiable. That, for me, is what it's all about.

"Our culture has accepted two lies: that if you disagree with someone's lifestyle you must hate them or are afraid of them, and that to love someone means that you must agree with everything they believe or do. Both are nonsense."

RICK WARREN

10

RICK WARREN

What Must We Do?

An Evangelical Perspective

THERE IS ALWAYS A DANGER in being the twenty-eighth speaker in a conference. What's left to say?

After hearing so many great speakers yesterday, I cancelled my dinner engagement last night to write a new message because most of what I had prepared to speak about was already covered by the speakers before me. I had prepared a message called "Why Marriage Matters," but I didn't want to repeat what you've already heard.

I had prepared to speak on how God reveals his presence and character through marriage, but that was eloquently explained by Cardinal Müller. I had also prepared to speak on the specific ways that our lives, our culture, and especially our children are damaged when we reject God's plan for marriage and sex; but *that* was eloquently explained by Pastor Arnold.

I had also prepared to speak about how gender ideologies confuse our identity and destroy our dignity – but, of course, Sister Prudence brilliantly explained that. I had prepared to speak about how the covenant of marriage and the act of sex parallel the intimate relationship that God wants to have with us, but my *former* friend Rabbi Sacks powerfully explained that. With every speaker, my speech kept getting shorter and shorter. So in conclusion, I now understand what our Lord Jesus felt when he said in John 10:8: "All who came before me are thieves and robbers"!

In Hebrews 13:4 we are given this clear command: "Marriage is to be honored by everyone."

Sadly, today, marriage is now dishonored by many. It is dismissed as an archaic, manmade tradition, denounced as an enemy of women, discouraged as a career-limiting choice, demeaned in movies and television, and delayed out of fear that it will limit one's personal freedom.

Today marriage is ridiculed, resented, rejected, and redefined. What are we going to do about this? The church cannot cower in silence! As you have heard, there is too much at stake.

So after hearing all that we've heard, I sat down and outlined an action plan of possible steps we might take

---

✦ REV. DR. RICHARD D. WARREN *is founder and senior pastor of Saddleback Church in Lake Forest, California. His book* The Purpose Driven Life *has sold thirty million copies and is the second most translated book in history, after the Bible. He hosted the Civil Forum on the Presidency (August 2008) with candidates McCain and Obama and gave the invocation at Obama's first presidential inauguration (January 2009). He initiated the P.E.A.C.E. Plan with the goal of involving Christians from every church in serving people in the areas of the greatest need globally. This work includes a major initiative to combat AIDS in Africa.*

after this colloquium ends. Rather than "Why Marriage Matters," my new title is "What Must We Do?" Just for fun, I put these action steps in alphabetical order:

A. Affirm the authority of God's Word.

We do not base our worldview on fads or feelings or opinions or political correctness. We build our lives on the unchanging truth of God's Word. Jesus affirmed, "Heaven and earth will pass away, but my words will never pass away." Isaiah affirmed that "the grass withers, and the flowers fade, but the word of God stands forever." David affirmed, "Your word, O Lord, is eternal. It stands firm in the heavens" (Ps. 119:89). Truth is still truth no matter who doubts it. I may deny the law of gravity but that doesn't change gravity. And just because we break God's laws, that does not invalidate them.

B. Believe what Jesus taught about marriage.

In Mark 10:6–9, Jesus quotes the Old Testament and gives us the Owner's Manual on Marriage. Many speakers have referred to this. Let me read it from the New Living Translation:

> God made them male and female from the beginning of creation. This explains why a man leaves his father and mother and is joined to his wife, and the two are united into one. Since they are no longer two but one, let no one split apart what God has joined together.

In this one passage Jesus gives us five convictions we must believe. First, gender is God's idea. God chose to make us either male or female. Our identity as either a man or woman is far deeper than a sociological construct, a psychological condition, or a personal preference. God created us male and female. Second, marriage is God's idea. He defines it, not us. It's not a manmade idea that we can toss away. Third, sex was created for marriage.

God created male and female body parts to naturally fit together. That's obvious. And they fit together for a purpose. They create life. Even if you disbelieve the Bible, every human body, and every living person, is a witness and testimony to God's intended purpose for sex. Sex was not created for recreation, but for the connection of a husband and wife and the procreation of life. If sex was only physical, unfaithfulness would not hurt so much; there is no "safe" sex because no condom can prevent a broken heart. Fourth, marriage is the union of a man and a woman. There are many other kinds of relationships, but those aren't marriage. Definitions matter. Fifth, marriage is to be permanent. Jesus repeats Genesis, adding, "What God joins together, no human being should separate." Marriage is meant to last a lifetime.

Today all five of these truths are dismissed and ridiculed. But a lie doesn't become truth, and wrong doesn't become right, and evil doesn't become good, just because it becomes popular.

C. *Celebrate healthy marriages.*

Be a proponent of what's right, rather than just being an opponent of what's wrong. We must offer an appealing alternative to the empty promises of the world. Celebrating and highlighting great marriages is the best defense of marriage. We will convert more opponents by being winsome and positive about the beauty and joy of marriage than by being negative about immorality. How? I have four suggestions for local churches:

1. *Use testimonies of happy marriages in your church services.* Both single adults and married couples are inspired more by example than by exhortation. They need to see the sermon in action. Having couples regularly share their journey with the whole

congregation will create a culture of marriage in the church. Remember, a marriage does not have to be perfect to be healthy.

2. *Do an annual "Renewal of Wedding Vows" service for your entire congregation.* We invite couples to dress up and do a processional. It is a very tender service; people weep for joy. It's a great model. For unmarried couples living together we announce it two months in advance so they can repent and take our required eight pre-marriage counseling courses.

3. *Publicly recognize and reward long-term marriages in your parishes.* Whatever gets rewarded gets repeated! If we want people to value marriage, we must reward it. Celebrate the sweetness and beauty of love that lasts a lifetime; we're wired to crave this.

4. *Continually point out the benefits of marriage.* When a culture claims to care about children, we must point out that children who grow up with both a mother and a father grow up healthier, happier, and stronger. They are less likely to fail in school, less likely to abuse drugs and alcohol, less likely to do jail time, and less likely to experience distress, depression, and thoughts of suicide. They are also less likely to perpetuate these problems to the next generation.

   When a culture claims to champion women, we must point out that women who marry and stay married have lower rates of depression, have a lower risk of being a victim of crime or violence, and have a higher net worth than those living with an unmarried man.

   When a culture claims to care for the poor, we must point out that the dissolution of marriages disproportionately hurts the poor. A single mother with children has never been a viable economic unit, and poor children get hurt the most by the economic consequences of divorce. Children who grow up without both mother and father are more likely to live their entire lives in poverty.

And what about men? Men who marry and stay married have fewer illnesses, fewer injuries, and live longer than single men. They earn more money and amass more net worth than single men with similar education and job histories, including men who live with unmarried women.

D. *Develop small group courses to support marriages.*
We've developed several of these at Saddleback, and small groups are one of the keys to our growth. We teach that as a couple, you should choose as your best friends other couples that are as committed to their marriage as you are to yours. Otherwise, you set up for failure.

E. *Engage every media to promote marriage.*
Right now, the church is being out-marketed by opponents of marriage. The minority view is getting the majority of media attention. Right now, Christians are known more for what we are against than what we are for. Whichever side tells the best stories wins.

We need more television shows and movies that portray joyful, committed married love.

We also must use media to question the cultural lies. For example, the media has conditioned our culture to believe the lie that sex is only exciting outside of marriage. We need tasteful movies and television shows that celebrate sex in marriage. Sex is not dirty. It is holy, and it is a gift to married couples. We need movies that teach the difference between love and lust. Love can always wait to give; lust can never wait to get.

As Christians, we need a cooperative media strategy for producing television shows, films, and YouTube videos and that portray the joys and benefits of a healthy marriage, and the hard work it takes to maintain a great marriage.

On a personal level I urge you to regularly use social media to mentor the next generation. I use nine channels.

F. *Face attackers with joy and winsomeness.*

Yes, there is a raging cultural battle. But the Bible says, "The weapons we fight with are not the weapons of the world." The Bible tells us to overcome evil with good and to bless those who curse you. Attackers are not the enemy; they are the mission field. Jesus died for them.

Our culture has accepted two lies: that if you disagree with someone's lifestyle you must hate them or are afraid of them, and that to love someone means that you must agree with everything they believe or do. Both are nonsense.

Over the past thirty-five years, I've trained over 400,000 pastors in 164 countries. Every church leader needs training in how to represent Christ when attacked. But it's a fact: if you stand courageously for the truth, you will be attacked. How do you stay winsome under attack?

First, remember your reward: "Blessed are you when people insult you, persecute you and falsely say all kinds of evil against you because of me. Rejoice and be glad, because great is your reward in heaven . . ." We must be willing to be ridiculed, and even to suffer, for the truth. Courage by its very nature often requires taking an unpopular stand. In his concluding message at the end of the Extraordinary Synod, the Holy Father said that we must avoid "the temptation to come down off the cross, to please the people, instead of staying on the cross fulfilling the will of the Father; the temptation to bow down to a worldly spirit instead of purifying it and bending it to the Spirit of God."

Second, live for an audience of One. Remember who we answer to at the end of the day.

On CNN I was asked, "Can you imagine ever changing your mind about gay marriage?" I said no. "Why?" I said, "Because I fear God's disapproval more than I fear your disapproval or society's." As Saint Peter has said, "We must obey God rather than men."

The only way to always be relevant is to be eternal. What is in style goes out of style; no revolution lasts. Every lie eventually crumbles under its own deception. Cultures rise and fall, cultures come and go, but the Word of God and the church of God continues. It isn't necessary to be on the right side of culture or the right side of history. It is just necessary to be on the right side!

In many ways, the debate over the definition of life, of sex, and of marriage is, in reality, a question of leadership. Who is going to lead? Will the church follow the crowd, or will the church lead the crowd? In Exodus 23:2 God says "Do not follow the crowd in doing wrong." Why? Because history shows that the majority is often wrong. The dustbins of history are stuffed with the conventional wisdom of cultures that proved false. Truth is not decided by a popularity contest.

G. Give people confidence.

Two Catholic leaders I respect have talked about this: Archbishop Kurtz told me, "We must restore confidence that even in a broken world a biblical marriage is attainable." And Cardinal Chaput has said, "Believers don't have the luxury of pessimism."

We must preach the good news about marriage with hope and faith, not doom and gloom. Instead of merely telling it like it is, pastors must tell it like it can be. We must show them how they can beat the odds. We must help couples imagine how good their marriages could be if they will make the effort to improve it. This is preaching for faith! Jesus said, "According to your faith it will be done to you."

We must help people see their primary identity is found in Christ and not in their sins or any other distinction. For example, Saddleback's Celebrate Recovery program differs from Alcoholics Anonymous. At AA meetings a person identifies himself as "I am an alcoholic," but in Celebrate Recovery, which we base on the Beatitudes of Jesus, a person says "I am a disciple of Christ who struggles with alcohol." That makes a huge difference in both theology and practice.

T. Teach the purposes of marriage. (I skipped to T because I'm out of time.)

You cannot value something until you understand its purpose. Anytime we forget God's intended purpose for any of his gifts, that gift will be misused, confused, abused, wasted, perverted, and even destroyed. This is true of your time, your money, your health, your freedom, your sexuality, and even marriage.

The Bible, primarily in Genesis, tells us that God created marriage for six purposes. We've discussed these in this conference, but let me just summarize them in a list:

1. *For the elimination of loneliness.* In Genesis 1:18 God tells Adam, "It is not good for man to be alone. I will make you a companion."

2. *For the expression of sex.* In Genesis 2:24 God says, "For this reason a man will leave his father and mother and be united to his wife, and they will become one flesh."

3. *For the multiplication of the human race.* In Genesis 1:28 God says, "Be fruitful and multiply and fill the earth." This is the only command humans have obeyed successfully. Seven billion of us prove it.

4. *For the protection and education of children.* In Ephesians 6:4 God says, "Fathers bring up your children in the nurture and the instruction of the Lord." Many speakers have already pointed out that children are hurt the most in a culture that devalues and dissolves marriage. I love *The Message* paraphrase of Malachi 2:15: "God, not you, made marriage. His Spirit inhabits even the smallest details of marriage. And what does he want from marriage? Children of God, that's what. So guard the spirit of marriage within you."

5. *For the perfection of our character.* First Corinthians 7:14 tells us "the husband is sanctified through his wife, and the wife is sanctified through her husband." A purpose of marriage to make us holy, not merely happy. It is the laboratory for learning to love. It's the school for learning sacrifice. It's the university for learning unselfishness. It's the lifelong course for becoming like Christ. If you are married, the number one tool God uses to shape you is your spouse!

6. *For the reflection of our union with Christ.* Ephesians 5:22–33 explains that marriage is a metaphor, a model of the mystery of Christ's love for his bride and body:

   > Husbands, love your wives, just as Christ loved the church and gave himself up for her to make her holy, cleansing her by the washing with water through the word, and to present her to himself as a radiant church, without stain or wrinkle or any other blemish, but holy and blameless. In this same

> way, husbands ought to love their wives as their own bodies. He who loves his wife loves himself. After all, no one ever hated their own body, but they feed and care for their body, just as Christ does the church – for we are members of his body. "For this reason a man will leave his father and mother and be united to his wife, and the two will become one flesh." This is a profound mystery – but I am talking about Christ and the church. However, each one of you also must love his wife as he loves himself, and the wife must respect her husband.

> This is the deepest meaning of marriage. This is the most profound purpose of marriage. This is the strongest reason marriage can only be between a man and a woman. No other relationship, including the parent-child relationship, can portray this intimate union. To redefine marriage would destroy the picture that God intends for marriage to portray. We cannot cave on this issue.

Jesus said there is no marriage in heaven. Why? Because in heaven we won't need any of the six purposes of marriage. In a perfect place, we won't need protection of children, or the perfection of character, or even the reflection of our union with Christ because we will experience the reality!

In closing, I want to encourage you to never give up and never give in. The church cannot be salt and light in a crumbling culture if it caves in to the sexual revolution and fails to provide a countercultural witness. It is a myth that we must give up biblical truth on sexuality and marriage in order to evangelize.

Twenty years ago I wrote *The Purpose Driven Church.* The subtitle of that book was "Growth without Compromising Your Message and Mission." I think that we've proved that is possible. Last month our local congregation baptized our 40,000th adult convert. Compromising truth has never grown anything. It only leads to decline and death, and I warn those flirting with this myth that it would be a terrible mistake for the church.

In the end we must be merciful to the fallen, show grace to the struggling, and be patient with the doubting. But when God's word is clear we must not and we cannot back up, back off, back down, or backslide from the truth.

The church must never be captivated by culture, manipulated by critics, motivated by applause, frustrated by problems, debilitated by distractions, or intimidated by evil. We must keep running the race with our eyes on the goal, not on those shouting from the sideline. We must be Spirit-led, purpose-driven, and mission-focused so that we cannot be bought, will not be compromised, and shall not quit until we finish the race. May God bless you and all who serve our Lord and Savior Jesus Christ!

"We are tired of what Pope Francis has referred to as 'the throwaway culture.' We are a large group of young people who don't want to see any more broken families and are fed up with seeing so much unnecessary suffering."

IGNACIO IBARZÁBAL

11

IGNACIO IBARZÁBAL

Global Education in Love

A Millennial Perspective

I AM FROM ARGENTINA, from the end of the world, and as you have seen through Pope Francis, we are used to several unusual things. Sometimes when I am on the train to work, I meet an old man playing the accordion up and down the carriages. He sings: "Only love can save the world."

I think that this phrase has great truth. Today I want to share with you what many young people are calling the "Rebellion of Solid Love." In fact I am part of Grupo Sólido, an organization of young people that promotes this rebellion in different countries, starting with Latin America and Spain. We have already reached numerous cities promoting the ideal of "solid love," which for us is identified with living romantic relationships in a generous way hoping to create sustainable families.

I said that we are fostering a rebellion. It happens that we are tired of what Pope Francis has referred to as "the throwaway culture." We are a large group of young people who don't want to see any more broken families and are fed up with seeing so much unnecessary suffering. That's why we are rebelling in the face of what we call "the crisis of unity."

The crisis of unity

We see that in so many aspects of our lives unity seems to be cherished. When we think of friendship, we want to be united to our friends. As well, we value unity when thinking about our siblings, about fraternity. In fact, one of the great literary works of Latin America, *Martín Fierro,* says: "For siblings to be united – this is the first law. If they fight among themselves, they are devoured by those outside." We may even consider how unity is cherished in politics. How often do we beg our politicians to set personal interests aside and heed the common good? Now when it comes to families, it seems that unity has lost its value. This points to a great paradox. Some years ago, Pope Benedict XVI affirmed in *Deus Caritas Est* that the paradigm of love among humans is romantic love. How did we come to lose sight of the value of unity in the most paradigmatic manifestation of love known to humanity?

In the end it seems that romantic relationships consist of uniting only to separate. As if separation,

---

✦ IGNACIO IBARZÁBAL *is the founder and president of Grupo Sólido, an organization based in Argentina that seeks to educate young adults about the nature of authentic love and marriage. A member of the Policy Strategy Group and The World We Want 2015, Ibarzábal is professor of family law at the Universidad Austral in Argentina. Previously, he was a visiting researcher at the University of Notre Dame Center for Ethics and Culture.*

fragmentation, and division were a solution to the fact that finding harmony is difficult, and that it is difficult to stay united. It is in the face of this aimless notion that we have set out our rebellion.

I will not bore you with statistics that you surely know much better than I do. We know the figures: unbearable levels of domestic violence, skyrocketing divorce statistics, and marriage dragged on the ground. We also know the impact that these realities have on children's and women's poverty, and in the long term, on older people as well. Let me only share an anecdote: A few years ago we went with our organization to give a workshop in a school in a very humble neighborhood in the city of Buenos Aires. We were working with a group of fifteen-year-old girls. We started the workshop by asking them two questions. The first was: Would you like to have a lifelong love? One hundred percent of them said yes. The second question was simple: Do you think this is possible? Eighty percent of them said no. We are talking about fifteen-year-old girls. Could there possibly be a more romantic or utopian demographic on the face of the earth than fifteen-year-old girls? Yet eighty percent of them said that they don't think it is possible to love one person for a lifetime.

Faced with this challenge, we cannot stay indifferent. We cannot remain on the sidelines while so many young people are tempted to lose hope about their most fundamental yearnings, about their dreams.

Global love education

We are here to change this reality. We are thus presented with a great challenge. How do we respond to this crisis of unity? I believe that there is an answer, and that it is to create and promote a true "global love education."

About a year ago at the World Youth Day, Pope Francis called on young people to "make a mess!" I don't know the impact this has had on the rest of the world, but in Argentina it was a tremendously mobilizing call. Today I want to share with you the way in which we interpret this call to "make a mess": promoting global love education. It is global because we want to go out and encounter diverse realities. Global because of the holistic view of the person implied. Global because of the use of new technologies.

Allow me to share with you how we are trying to do it. First, we are seeking to truly serve others, including families. I think we have wasted far too much time. We have wasted time pretending to listen without truly doing so. We have been caught up in the incidental rather than the essential. We have been defending our ideas instead of sharing in service of others. It is time for us to stop wasting time. Today is the day and now is the hour. The path is simple: we must learn to listen more, to stand side-by-side with other people, and to understand why they are suffering. Only then can we begin to reestablish our proposal.

Now, for this proposal to take shape, we must seek further clarity, reasoned from another base. Our clarity must be centred on what is understood by others, not only what we say. In fact, Saint Paul said in the First Letter to the Corinthians: "I would rather speak five understandable words to help others than ten thousand words in an unknown language" (14:19). If we open ourselves to listen, we can find ourselves greatly surprised. For example, about two years ago, Richard Weissbourd, a professor at the Harvard Graduate School of Education, concerned about what he defines as an "epic abdication of responsibility" by schools to provide love education, conducted a survey consulting hundreds of young people about what most worries them about sexual and affective education. Seventy percent of them answered that they would like to receive education on how to develop mature relationships.

Always be ready to explain

A second relevant task is to be ready to explain our hopes (Eph. 1:18). I look at all of you and I see diverse traditions united in service of families. Seeing you, I am certain that we haven't received a check with insufficient funds. On the contrary, we have a blank check, full of richness to offer to the world. It is time that we come out to share it in a positive and creative way.

I can assume that many of you are concerned by the current state of marriage. Certainly, so am I, as are a great number of young people. In our day and age there is far too much uncertainty. In fact, I was reminded before coming here of a conversation that I recently had with a friend over coffee. I recall that when we met she had been in a relationship for quite some time but had doubts about whether or not to get married. She said that while she found herself in a sort of "social inertia," she saw no practical advantage to marriage, and above all, didn't want to repeat her parents' mistakes. Getting to the roots of these worries, at one point she said a phrase that left an impression on me: "Deep down, I feel that marriage destroys everything that it touches."

This is the vision that many young people have of marriage. With this as a starting point, I ask myself what would happen if we went out to the world in a creative way to demonstrate what the essence of marriage is about. What would happen if we showed that marriage is a privileged context for choosing someone to love? What would happen if we showed that it is not a hollow shell? If we showed that, far from being a formality, it is one of the most significant actions that we could undertake in our lives? The image of the wedding rings expressed by Karol Wojtyła in *The Jewelers' Shop* comes to mind. These small pieces of precious metal weigh together "the whole existence of man and his destiny." It is clear that our life is at stake in marriage, and that is why it is one of the most important and significant events that we can experience in our lifetime. This is the message that we have to go out and share with the world, and we should do it with confidence, since it is a great one. Now, the big challenge is how to communicate it.

Making it accessible

This is perhaps our greatest challenge. Putting ourselves at the service of others and showing the reasons for our hope is necessary but not sufficient. What the world needs is for us to make this hope accessible, and within everyone's reach. This is what "global love education" is about.

Today, children are no longer educated merely by their parents and at school. They are educated by their parents, school, by radio, television, the Internet, Facebook, Twitter, Instagram, Whatsapp, and the list goes on. We have to learn to be savvy in this new cultural context. If we truly want to promote a global education in love, and if we want to solve this crisis of unity, we need to be bold enough to take this path. We have to challenge ourselves to fill these new platforms with millions of micro-messages. If not, we will fall short.

This must imply a new paradigm. I am not referring to a pair of isolated initiatives. I am not speaking of one particular parish activity. I want to invite all of you to a greater awareness that the world is the same, but we need a new map to navigate it. Columbus' maps won't do us much good anymore. We cannot rely on what was mapped out ten, fifteen, or twenty years ago to provide sex and love education. We need new forms of navigation, and we need to reach new frontiers. We need to think outside the box. This is what it means to make this proposal accessible to the world.

This is what the "Rebellion of Solid Love" is about. We have been feeding this rebellion for years. A few moments ago, while listening to Pope Francis – naturally quite moved – I was thinking of the opportunity that the current crisis provides us. I believe that this crisis of unity exists, that it is a reality, and that we have to face it. Global love education is the answer. It implies that we place ourselves at the service of others, explaining the reason for our hope while making it accessible to others. This rebellion, which at this point is little more than a promise, may sooner than later transform into a profound change of paradigm, into a revolution. This is why I call on all of you to remain open, to stay creative and positive. Because this promise of rebellion can become the reality of a revolution – a revolution of personalist love, of responsible love, of solid love. Because, as we mustn't forget, quoting the musician of the Buenos Aires train, "Only love can save the world."

"Human life is all about relationship. It cannot become complete unless it fuses into a fuller integrated bond which includes both man and woman, husband and wife, mother and child, grandmother and child, and male and female colleagues in vocation."

KALA ACHARYA

12

KALA ACHARYA

Only Half without the Other

A Hindu Perspective

BY THE TERM "Hindu perspective" I mean the views that are accorded authenticity, being based on the scriptures – mainly the Vedas and the *Upaniṣads,* which form the last portion of the Vedas, and the *Smṛtis,* that is, the law books, the *Purāṇas,* the *Rāmāyaṇa,* and the *Mahābhārata.*

The *Ṛgveda,* the ancient scripture of Hinduism, declares that it is the wife who makes a man's dwelling a sweet home.[1] The *Atharvaveda* says that all the members of a family should live in concord, and that the wife should converse with her husband in sweet and peaceful words.[2] The *Śatapatha Brāhmaṇa* states, "The wife is indeed half of one's self; one becomes complete only when one gets married and procreates."[3] The *Bṛhadāraṇyaka Upaniṣad,* while describing the creation of the world, says:

> In the beginning, all this was verily the Self, in the form of a person. Observing around, he did not behold

> anything other than himself. . . . Verily, he did not at all feel delighted. . . . He grew as big as a man and a woman closely embracing each other. He divided this very body into two. Therefrom husband and wife came into being. . . . This body of oneself is like a half fragment of a full two-celled seed. Therefore this void is filled by the wife indeed. He united with her. And therefrom human beings were born.[4]

In Vedic times, woman's social position was by no means one of slavish submission to masculine power. It has been said, "A house is not a house; only the wife is called a house" (*Jāyedastam*). The Sanskrit word for householder, *gṛhastha,* means a man who stays with his wife. According to scriptural injunctions a man cannot perform any rite unless he is accompanied by his wife.

In addition to scriptures, in the iconography of the Hindu deities we find a reflection of the laudable position of the female power. Not only are goddesses such as Durgā, Kāli, and Pārvatī worshipped as *Śakti* – the Energy – but also the complete union of male and female

---

✦ KALA ACHARYA, PHD, *has been the director of K.J. Somaiya Bharatiya Sanskriti Peetham Cultural and Research Institute in India since its inception in 1989. During her tenure the institute has been developed as a center for interreligious dialogue between Hinduism, Christianity, and Islam, and offers post-graduate programs in Sanskrit, yoga, philosophy, and history. The author of several books, Acharya represented Hinduism in international interreligious meetings organized by the Pontifical Council for Interreligious Dialogue. She has been a member of the Secretariat of the Congress of the Leaders of World and Traditional Religions in Kazakhstan and was appointed as an ambassador for the Parliament of World Religions in 2009.*

power is depicted through the image of *Ardhanārīnaṭeśvara* (half-man and half-woman form) which symbolizes Lord Śiva and *Śakti* as an inseparable pair. The tradition considers woman as *Śakti* and declares that Lord Śiva is rather powerless if he is not accompanied by the goddess Pārvatī, who is his consort and energy.

Religious Aspect

The Hindu scriptures speak about different dimensions of the man-woman relationship. "Daṃpatī," a hymn from the *Ṛgveda,* is about the life of a couple. The entire hymn has a sacrificial tone. It tells us how a couple performing religious rites live happily, how they are gifted with sons and daughters, and how they lead a long span of life in prosperity. The hymn runs:

> Husband and wife in sweet accord
>   Give milk oblations to the gods
> And press and strain *soma.*
>   They acquire a plenteous store of food.
> They come united to the altar.
>   Their rewards never lessen.
> They do not wander from the gods
>   Or seek to hide their favors granted.
> Thus they acquire great glory.
>   With sons and daughters at their side
> They live a good span of years.
>   Both decked with precious gold,
> Devoted to sacrifice, gathering wealth,
>   They serve the immortal and honor the gods,
> United in mutual love.[5]

In Hindu scriptures the union of man and woman was accorded a central place in the economy of the universe, as they are the symbol of cosmic polarity. Marriage should not be considered only as a legal contract. It is the human counterpart of dualities in the cosmic order. Marriage is tuning to the cosmic harmony. The hymn about marriage in the *Ṛgveda,* and also this one in the *Atharvaveda,* use cosmic and metaphysical terms to indicate this significance:

> By truth is the earth supported.
> By the sun is the heaven supported.
> By cosmic order the Āditya stand.
> And the moon is set upon the sky.[6]

Marriage is a sacrifice (*yajña,* which implies both a sacred rite and willingness to sacrifice one's happiness for the other.)[7] A single man or a single woman is not a complete person. They are halves only, representing an existential split in the existing order of the world and becoming complete only in their union. Hindus believe that God makes the gift of the bride to the bridegroom. The following Vedic mantra, in which the bridegroom addresses the bride, reveals this idea:

> I hold your hand for begetting excellent children, and I will be holding your hand till you attain old age. Bhaga, Aryamā, Savitā, Indra, and other gods have presented you to me for observing the household austerities.[8]

The husband addresses his wife with the following words: "May Viṣṇu make you fit for lovemaking. May you attain progeny by the grace of Prajāpati, the Creator. May Tvaṣṭā fashion the limbs of the child."[9]

Marriage is meant to continue the family line. Love between the couple is based on mutual trust. In the *Atharvaveda* the husband says to the wife:

Sweet be the glances we exchange,
  Our faces showing true concord.
Enshrine me in your heart and
  Let one spirit dwell within us.[10]

The poet Kalidāsa says that friendship develops between two persons if they take seven steps together.[11] There is a lot of significance in the seven steps taken by the bride and the bridegroom together during the ritual of marriage. The bridegroom says:

> May you be my associate. May we become friends. May we attain the benefits of friendship. May I not be separated from your friendship. Let us take the oath together. Let us love each other. May we both attain luster. May we entertain good thoughts. Let us enjoy the food and attain strength. Let us place our family life on a firm footing. Let us plan and carry out our undertakings and austerities together. Let us be united in mind. . . . I am the sky and you are the earth. I am the life force and you are the bearer of that life force. I am the mind and you are the speech. May you be cooperative in begetting male progeny. May we attain prosperity and excellent progeny.[12]

During the marriage ceremony, the husband says to his wife: "May you follow me, O sweet-speaking lady. May you mount the stone; may you be steady like the stone."[13] This ritual of standing on the stone indicates that the woman will not leave her husband and his house even in adversities. Then the husband takes his wife around the house, introduces her to his relatives, and pronounces some mantras for general welfare. The bride is blessed thus:

> Happy be thou and prosper with thy children here. Be vigilant to rule thy household in this home. Closely unite thy body with this man, thy lord. So shall ye, full of years, address the assembly.[14]

> Be ye not parted. Dwell ye here; reach the full span of human life. Sport and play with sons and grandsons, rejoicing in your own house.[15]

The *Atharvaveda* speaks not only about the compatibility of man and woman, but also about the ideal of "union of hearts and minds and freedom from hate" amongst all members of a family. To achieve this concord, it admonishes family members to love one another as a cow loves her newborn calf.[16]

Compatibility requires some difference, so that the two come together. The *Atharvaveda* speaks of:

> The majesty and the luster in the male,
> In the hero and the steed,
> In the wild beast and in the elephant,
> And the radiance that is in the maiden.[17]

The *Smṛtis* – the law books of the Hindus – also have abundant references showing the harmonious relationship of man and woman as bringing favorable results. The *Manusmṛti* says that the family where the wife and the husband satisfy each other is always endowed with well-being.[18]

The Indian tradition conceives power as feminine and speaks about its three aspects. These are willpower *(icchāśakti)*, power of knowledge *(jñānaśakti)*, and power to act *(kriyāśakti)*. These three are the cause of any actual or symbolic creation on the earth. We find that in Sanskrit all the qualities which express sublime sentiments, refined and tender emotions such as compassion *(karuṇā),* pity *(dayā),* forgiveness *(kṣamā),* and intelligence (*prajñā*), are used in the feminine gender. Also, qualities such as affection *(vātsalya),* having abundant fertility *(bahuprasavaśīlatvam),* and beauty *(śobhā)* are common to women and the earth. The earth is the role model for women, as she forgives every kind of wrong done to her.

The qualities mentioned above are needed for key posts in the corporate world. So nowadays we find a trend of formation of teams which consists of both men and women, for the reason that their compatibility can give more positive results. For example, abundant fertility in this context means the power to conceive multiple projects. The *Ardhanārīnaṭeśvara* form of Lord Śiva combining one half of male and the other of female indicates how two coming together work for perfection.

In the epic *Raghuvaṃśa,* King Aja, while lamenting over his wife's death, is not shy of articulating his dedication to his wife:

> Never before have I wronged thee even in thought; why hast thou forsaken me? Lord of the Earth, indeed, only in name, have I been; but to thee alone I give my heart's real love.[19]

This shows that dedication for a couple was mutual. The wife used to carry multiple responsibilities. For example, King Aja's wife, Indumatī, is described as the mistress of his home, counselor, friend, witness of his intimate moments, and his beloved pupil in all the fine arts.[20]

Hindu iconography also sheds light on the infinite and multitasking ability of the female principle when the goddess Durgā is depicted as having eight arms *(aṣṭabhujā)* whereas all the male deities are depicted as having a maximum of four arms.

Philosophical Aspect

The Sāṃkhya – one of the orthodox schools of Indian philosophy – depicts a model of realistic dualism which posits the doctrines of *Prakṛti* (female doctrine – matter) and *Puruṣa* (male doctrine – the soul). *Puruṣa* is an intelligent, eternal, conscious, neutral, passive, and unmanifest principle.[21] *Prakṛti* is an insentient, eternal, and active principle. She is constituted of three qualities: goodness, passion, and inertia. When these qualities are in equilibrium the process of world creation is at a standstill. The contact of *Prakṛti* and *Puruṣa* affects this equilibrium and consequently world-creation takes place.

The relation between *Puruṣa* and *Prakṛti* is of interdependence. From *Prakṛti* evolves this world, full of enjoyments *(bhoga)*; at the same time, she has a design for the realization of the spiritual ends of *Puruṣa*. The mere presence of *Puruṣa* causes creative power in the shy *Prakṛti,* who produces the manifold world. The union of the two is compared with a lame person on the shoulder of a blind man, which helps both of them reach the desired destination due to their cooperation and also helps them overcome their shortcomings. *Prakṛti* manifests out of compassion for *Puruṣa* to facilitate his liberation, just as mother's milk oozes forth out of compassion for her child.[22] This cosmic design of creation is the model for man and woman in earthly life.

Practical Aspect

The last few centuries have brought a great awakening amongst women regarding their status. The growing political awareness amongst women has inspired their active participation in local administrative bodies. Working conditions for women are improving. Those who are not earning have shed their inferiority complex and have become confident about what they contribute to their families and society. The trend of couples working in unison with integrity to serve the community is on rise. To mention a few examples from India, we can refer to Dr. Prakash and Manda Amte, who were awarded the Magsaysay Award for Community Leadership in 2008 for their philanthropic work amongst the Madia Gonds, a tribal community in Maharashtra and the neighboring states of Andhra Pradesh and Madhya Pradesh. Dr. Abhay and Rani Bang are social activists who have worked for healthcare for underprivileged people. They have reduced neonatal mortality rates in one of the most poverty-stricken areas in the world. Mahatma Jotiba and Savitribal Phule (nineteenth century) were activists, thinkers, and social reformers from Maharashtra who pioneered women's education. They also worked for removal of the caste system and untouchability, and for the dignity of women, especially widows. N. R. Narayana Murthy, the famous IT industrialist, and his wife, Sudha Murthy, are famous for their invaluable contributions to society.

The complementarity of man and woman is the perfect blending of the emotional and the intellectual quotient, which results in a perfectly balanced attitude of human nature needed for crucial moments. The concord of men and women working together unfolds a panorama of a marvelously broad horizon. Those who have awakened to this force of togetherness have advanced a long way and beckon to us, exemplifying the complementary nature of a relationship based on pure and selfless service, faith, and dedication.

Human life is all about relationship. It cannot become complete unless it fuses into a fuller integrated bond that includes both: man and woman, husband and wife, mother and child, grandmother and child, and male and female colleagues in vocation. Of these, the relationship between husband and wife represents the most intimate partnership. A Vedic mantra asks woman to stand by her husband in sun and shower and lead him to spiritual gain. This speaks about how a woman becomes a cause of worldly and spiritual growth of man:

> Hoping for love, children, fortune, wealth,
> And by being always behind
> Thy husband in his life's vocation,
> Gird thou up for immortality.[23]

1. *Ṛgveda 3.53.4.*
2. *Atharvaveda 3.30.1–2.*
3. *Śatapatha Brāhmaṇa 5.2.1.10.*
4. Brihadaranyaka Upanishad *1.4.1–3.*
5. *Ṛgveda 8. 31. 5–9.*
6. *Atharvaveda 14.1.1.*
7. *Taittirīya Brāhmaṇa 2, 2.2.6.*
8. *Ṛgveda 10.85.36.*
9. *Ṛgveda 10.184.1.*
10. *Atharvaveda 7.36.*
11. Kalidāsa, *Kumārasaṃbhava 5.39.*
12. *Āpastaṃba Mantrapāṭha* 1.3.14.
13. *Āpastaṃba Mantrapāṭha* 1.5.1.
14. *Ṛgveda* 10.85.27.
15. *Ṛgveda* 10.85.42.
16. *Atharvaveda* 3.30.
17. *Atharvaveda* 12.1.25.
18. *Manusmṛti* 3.60.
19. Kalidāsa, *Raghuvaṃśa* 8.52.
20. Kalidāsa, *Raghuvaṃśa* 8.67.
21. Haribhadra, *Ṣaḍdarśanasamuccaya* 41.
22. Īśvarakṛṣṇa, *Sāṃkhyakārikā,* 60.
23. *Atharvaveda* 14.1.42.

"God has called us, the church, to a sacred duty to defend the innocents and the disadvantaged, the children and the poor. . . . We in the black church and all people of faith must exemplify strong, stable marriages founded on God's principle of holy matrimony between one man and one woman. And we must promote the same among the faithful. As we are true to this calling, God will move."

JACQUELINE C. RIVERS

13

JACQUELINE C. RIVERS

God Has Brought Us to This Place

A Pentecostal Perspective

I AM PLEASED TO SPEAK to you as a follower of Jesus Christ for forty years, a leader in the black church in the United States, a daughter of the African diaspora, a Harvard-trained sociologist, a wife, and the mother of two young adults.

Something precious was stolen from blacks in the United States during slavery, a blessing from the hand of the Creator himself: the right of a man and a woman to be joined in holy matrimony. Under slavery, men and women were not permitted to have legally binding, permanent unions. Despite this, my ancestors longed to participate in the blessing of divinely sanctioned marriage. This yearning was demonstrated in their striving to be faithful to each other even under the harsh conditions of slavery. It was evident from the large numbers who were legally wed as soon as possible, immediately after emancipation.

The gift from God that these enslaved men and women sought was marriage. Marriage is a permanent bond between one man and one woman that provides the deepest levels of emotional and sexual fidelity and exclusivity. The resulting conjugal bond creates unity of husband and wife at every level: physical, emotional, volitional, and spiritual. "For this reason a man shall leave his father and his mother, and be joined to his wife; and they shall become one flesh" (Gen. 2:24).

Despite the determined pursuit of marital unions by freed people, enduring patterns of non-normative male-female relationships had been created by the devastating experience of slavery. These bore bitter fruit in the twenty-five-percent out-of-wedlock birth rate that prompted the Moynihan Report in 1965. The Moynihan Report was an examination of the pathologies created by the explosion of father-absent households among the black poor in the United States. Though the report recommended the creation of programs that would promote healthy families among impoverished blacks, it elicited an outpouring of outrage at the assertion that stable marriages were necessary for the flourishing of the black community.

✦ JACQUELINE C. RIVERS, PHD, *the director of the Seymour Institute for Black Church and Policy Studies, earned her doctorate in African-American Studies and Sociology at Harvard University. She is a doctoral fellow in the Multidisciplinary Program in Inequality & Social Policy at the Harvard Kennedy School. She was the founder and executive director of MathPower, a leading community-based nonprofit in Boston for mathematics education reform in urban schools. From 2001 to 2004 she served as executive director for the National TenPoint Leadership Foundation.*

As a result little action was taken to rectify these problems. Fifty years later the out-of-wedlock birth rate among blacks in the United States has soared to over seventy percent, a level at which it has stood for roughly a decade. The material, moral, and spiritual consequences are precisely what Moynihan predicted they would be: devastating for the community.

Black children have suffered the most as a result of the decline of marriage in the black community. The deleterious effects of being raised in female-headed households have been well documented. Children growing up in such households experience higher rates of poverty. These children underperform in school: they earn lower scores on verbal and math achievement tests and lower grades in their courses. They have more behavioral problems and higher rates of chronic health and psychiatric disorders. Adolescents and young adults raised without stable families experience elevated risks of teenage childbearing, of dropping out of high school, of being incarcerated, and of being idle (being neither employed nor in school). Yet even in the midst of this disarray, men and women still long for marriage. Research shows that though marriage has declined among poor women from different racial backgrounds, they, no less than affluent women, desire to be married even as they bear children out of wedlock.

Today, marriage faces new threats as the divinely established order of marriage between one man and one woman is challenged. Across the United States and Europe sexual partnerships between persons of the same sex are being legally recognized as "marriages," thus abolishing in law the principle of marriage as a conjugal union and reducing it to nothing other than sexual or romantic companionship or domestic partnership. The unavoidable message is a profoundly false and damaging one: that children do not need a mother and a father in a permanent, complementary bond.

To insist on the truth that neither mothers nor fathers are expendable is not to dishonor anyone's dignity. Every human being is beloved and precious in God's sight. The mere issue of an individual's sexual inclinations (or even sinful practices) cannot alter this. God loves all of us, and reaches out in love to sinners. Furthermore, as Christians and people of faith we are commanded to love each of our neighbors as ourselves. Therefore, we embrace all people, regardless of their struggles. However, though all people are created equal, all sexual practices are not.

As with the reaction to the Moynihan Report, those who decry the erosion of marriage are reviled. Christians who stand against these developments are in some cases under threat of losing their jobs and their businesses. Those who promote what they call marriage equality have unjustly appropriated the language and the mantle of the black struggle in the United States, the civil rights movement. But there can be no equivalence between blacks' experience of slavery and oppression and the circumstances of homosexuals. And as with the Moynihan Report, the terrible social consequences of these developments await us. But God is not mocked. He is the almighty God and will advance his plan for conjugal flourishing.

God has called us, the church, to a sacred duty to defend the innocents and the disadvantaged, the children and the poor, since he instructs us: "Religion that God our Father accepts as pure and faultless is this: to look after orphans and widows in their distress and to keep oneself from being polluted by the world" (James 1:27). We must relentlessly police ourselves, whether we are the black church or Roman Catholic, Muslim, or Orthodox Jew, to ensure that no predators among us take advantage of these innocents. We must deal unsparingly with religious leaders who aid such predators. All of us, especially the Roman Catholic Church, must collaborate with the authorities to prosecute them to the full extent of the law. In addition, we in the black church and all people of faith must exemplify strong, stable marriages, founded on God's principle of holy matrimony between one man and one woman. And we must promote the same among the faithful. As we are true to this calling, God will move.

In the depths of slavery God moved to free oppressed blacks. He raised up black abolitionists such as Sojourner Truth to carry the banner of freedom. God raised up and transformed a leader, Abraham Lincoln, to bring an end to the horrors of slavery.

Our God is omnipotent: he not only ended slavery, but eight decades later he moved again in the southern United States to destroy a new system of oppression that had replaced the old one. In the civil rights movement God called the black church to brave fire hoses and attack dogs and face down police brutality. God called a man, Martin Luther King Jr., to end racial tyranny.

Brothers and sisters, God can and will do it again. He is calling us to a global movement to promote the correct definition of marriage. Already God is moving to protect his divinely instituted structure of the family. In France God raised up hundreds of thousands of people to protest the legalization of so-called homosexual marriage. Right here in Rome, God called African bishops to oppose language that would undermine the biblical model for marriage and perhaps negatively impact pastoral practice.

God is refining and purifying us through this struggle. He has provided an opportunity for us to be a witness to the world of his supernatural power and his compassion. God is calling us to stand, in humility and love, against the movement to destroy marriage. God is calling us to defend innocent children whose futures are at risk. God is calling the Roman Catholic Church to stand firm for the biblical definition of marriage. True compassion cannot be practiced at the expense of sacred truth.

God our Father has brought us to this place, this day, to join in unity across faiths and around the world to defend the divine plan for marriage. Together, under God, we are stronger than those who would destroy the divine order for marriage. Together, under God, we vastly outnumber those who oppose God's plan. Together, under God, we will see him triumph, restoring a divinely inspired understanding of marriage.

"Though yin and yang look opposite to each other, they can't exist independently. . . . If there is no yin, yang can't appear alone. Likewise, if there is no yang, yin won't exist. That's the thought of coexistence, complementarity, and reciprocity. They form a perfect unity with two in one."

TSUI-YING SHENG

14

TSUI-YING SHENG

The Union of Yin and Yang

A Taoist Perspective

IT'S MY HONOR AND PLEASURE to be here from Taiwan to share with you my thoughts on the complementarity of yin and yang.

The concept of yin (陰) and yang (陽) originated from the ancient Chinese people's view of nature. Ancient Chinese people believed that everything in the universe has these two relative natural aspects and phenomena simultaneously, such as night and day, moon and sun, black and white, earth and sky, female and male, and so on. As we can see, they exist around us authentically. The theory of yin and yang has penetrated into all aspects of traditional Chinese culture, including religion, philosophy, calendar, medicine, architecture, geomancy, and so forth.

The concept of yin and yang is one of the important dogmas of Taoism. The canon *Laozi* (道德經), written by one of the Chinese Taoist philosophers, says everything under the sun is born of both yin and yang. Single yin or solitary yang is sterile. Nothing can be born only of single yin or solitary yang.

Let's take a look at the picture of the symbols of yin and yang. We call it "figure of the ultimate female and male" (*Taiji Yin-yang Tu,* 太極陰陽圖). The outside big circle in the picture is divided into two halves by a soft and smooth curve in the middle. The white half on the left is yang, and the black on the right is yin. Yang has a black dot in it while yin has a white one. It means they embrace and contain each other. They look like two fish nestling up to each other. So we also call them "female and male fish" (yin-yang fish, 陰陽魚).

Taiji Yin-yang Tu, 太極陰陽圖

Though yin and yang look like opposites, they can't exist independently. They embrace and coordinate each other, and also facilitate each other. One cannot exist or be defined without the other. If there is no yin, yang can't appear alone. Likewise, if there is no yang, yin won't exist. That's the thought of coexistence, complementarity, and reciprocity. They form a perfect unity with two in one.

The energy of yin and yang is circulating and dynamic. When yang is stronger, the opposite will be weaker to redress the balance of the energy, and vice versa, so as to maintain the completeness of the big circle. It's a kind of

---

✦ TSUI-YING SHENG *is a lecturer of Taoist Life Education at Fu Jen Catholic University, Taiwan, where she is also a PhD candidate in Religious Studies.*

vital and sustained relationship. Life grows and activates during the circulation of these two types of energy.

Therefore, this idea has also been applied to the characters of woman and man, as well as to the role of wife and husband in marriage. The whole big circle stands for a family. It consists of two major parts. The white fish is the man, husband and father, and the black fish is the woman, wife and mother. Each of the two contains some of the other. They both have to be considerate and support each other to keep the family whole. The relationship between them is smooth and integrated. Through incessant interaction and communication, equilibrium can be maintained. Without equilibrium between the man and the woman, there can be no harmonious and successful marriage, not to mention peaceful or prosperous lives.

My husband and I have learned the importance of the integrity of a family since we were very young. We have been taught that "a man should get married on coming of age, and so should a woman." In the Chinese traditional view of value, to procreate and to continue the family name is one of the basic responsibilities in our lives. And having a happy and complete family, which consists of a man, a woman, and children, is the supreme well-being in the world. We feel proud of having fulfilled this responsibility and task. And we enjoy it.

Did we have quarrels in our daily life? Sure we did. Since we are only ordinary mortals, we sometimes made mistakes and had different opinions. Every time we had a quarrel about something, either my husband or I would just keep silent after a few words. Then, in a very short time, we would find an opportunity to show our kindness to each other by just a simple smile or a cup of coffee.

A little talk about our children is usually an effectual subject at such a moment, because they remind us of our duty of being their models; we also know that there is no hate between two loving people.

As we all know, a family's development depends on the efforts of every member in it. My husband and I always try to stand in the each other's shoes to help make the family function smoothly and successfully. When he is busy doing his work, I handle most of the housework. When I have to sit at my desk to finish some writing, he takes charge of the housekeeping without thinking. It just happens naturally.

Those are some of the concrete representations of the complementary union of man and woman in marriage. Obviously, they correspond to the union and complementarity of yin and yang in the universe.

There is one more thing that I would like to share with you. My husband and I have two children, a handsome twenty-eight-year-old boy and a pretty twenty-six-year-old girl. We think that children have the right to complete family love coming from their father and mother. Just like most parents in the world do, we have always tried to take good care of our children. Their laughing really activates our lives and our family life. Now it's their turn to find their other half, to organize their family, and to carry on the responsibilities of maintaining the vitality of our family and the flourishing of human society.

"I have become a better person as I have loved and lived with her. We have been complementary beyond anything I could have imagined. . . . I realize now that we grew together into one – slowly lifting and shaping each other, year by year. As we absorbed strength from each other, it did not diminish our personal gifts. Our differences combined as if they were designed to create a better whole. Rather than dividing us, our differences bound us together."

HENRY B. EYRING

15

HENRY B. EYRING

To Become as One

A Mormon Perspective

I AM GRATEFUL TO BE INVITED to be a witness at this colloquium. I am especially grateful for the opportunity to give evidence that a man and a woman, united in marriage, have a transcendent power to create happiness for themselves, for their family, and for the people around them.

I am an eyewitness of the power of the union of a man and a woman in marriage to produce happiness for each other and for their family. The evidence I offer is personal, yet I trust my recital may trigger in your memories what you have seen that would point to a general truth beyond the experience of one couple and one family.

The evidence I offer begins when I was a single man, living alone without any family near me. I thought I was happy and content. I was a doctoral student at Harvard University in Cambridge, Massachusetts. My research work was going well, I was serving others through my church, and I found time to play tennis often.

An assignment in my church took me to a morning meeting in a grove of trees in New Hampshire. As the meeting ended, I saw in the crowd a young woman. I had never seen her before, but the feeling came over me that she was the best person I had ever seen. That evening she walked into our church meeting in Cambridge. Another thought came to my mind with great power: "If I could only be with her, I could become every good thing I ever wanted to be." I said to the man sitting next to me, "Do you see that girl? I would give anything to marry her."

We were married a year after I first saw her. The wedding ceremony was in a temple of The Church of Jesus Christ of Latter-day Saints. The words spoken in the ceremony included a promise that we might be husband and wife in this life and for eternity. The promise included that whatever descendants we might have would be bound to us forever if we lived worthy of that happiness. We were promised that after this life, we could continue to enjoy whatever loving family sociality we could create in life.

✦ PRESIDENT HENRY B. EYRING *is First Counselor in the First Presidency of The Church of Jesus Christ of Latter-day Saints. He was named to the church's Quorum of the Twelve Apostles in 1995. He has also served as church commissioner of education and as president of Ricks College in Rexburg, Idaho (now Brigham Young University–Idaho). President Eyring earned an MBA and PhD in Business Administration from Harvard Business School. A former member of the US Air Force, President Eyring and his wife, Kathleen, have six children.*

My wife and I believed those promises, and we wanted that happiness. So we acted to make it possible through the great variety of circumstances of life. There was sickness and health, struggle and some prosperity, the births of six children, and eventually the births of thirty-one grandchildren. Yet with all the changes, there have been consistencies since that wedding day more than fifty-two years ago.

Most remarkable to me has been the fulfillment of the hope I felt the day I met my wife. I have become a better person as I have loved and lived with her. We have been complementary beyond anything I could have imagined. Her capacity to nurture others grew in me as we became one. My capacity to plan, direct, and lead in our family grew in her as we became united in marriage. I realize now that we grew together into one – slowly lifting and shaping each other, year by year. As we absorbed strength from each other, it did not diminish our personal gifts.

Our differences combined as if they were designed to create a better whole. Rather than dividing us, our differences bound us together. Above all, our unique abilities allowed us to become partners with God in creating human life. The happiness that came from our becoming one built faith in our children and grandchildren that marriage could be a continuing source of satisfaction for them and their families.

You have seen enough unhappiness in marriages and families to ask why some marriages produce happiness while others create unhappiness. Many factors make a difference, but one stands out to me. Where there is selfishness, natural differences of men and women often divide. Where there is unselfishness, differences become complementary and provide opportunities to help and build each other. Spouses and family members can lift each other and ascend together if they care more about the interests of the other than their own interests.

If unselfishness is the key to complementary marriage between a man and a woman, we know what we must do to help create a renaissance of successful marriages and family life. We must find ways to lead people to a faith that they can replace their natural self-interest with deep and lasting feelings of charity and benevolence. With that change, and only then, will people be able to make the hourly unselfish sacrifices necessary for a happy marriage and family life – and to do it with a smile.

The change that is needed is in people's hearts more than in their minds. The most persuasive logic will not be enough unless it helps soften hearts. For instance, it is important for men and women to be faithful to a spouse and a family. But in the heat of temptation to betray their trust, only powerful feelings of love and loyalty will be enough.

That is why the following guidelines are in "The Family: A Proclamation to the World," issued in 1995 by the First Presidency and Quorum of the Twelve Apostles of The Church of Jesus Christ of Latter-day Saints:

> Husband and wife have a solemn responsibility to love and care for each other and for their children. "Children are a heritage of the Lord" (Ps. 127:3). Parents have a sacred duty to rear their children in love and righteousness, to provide for their physical and spiritual needs, and to teach them to love and serve one another, observe the commandments of God, and be law-abiding citizens wherever they live. Husbands and wives – mothers and

> fathers – will be held accountable before God for the discharge of these obligations.
>
> The family is ordained of God. Marriage between man and woman is essential to his eternal plan. Children are entitled to birth within the bonds of matrimony, and to be reared by a father and a mother who honor marital vows with complete fidelity. Happiness in family life is most likely to be achieved when founded upon the teachings of the Lord Jesus Christ. Successful marriages and families are established and maintained on principles of faith, prayer, repentance, forgiveness, respect, love, compassion, work, and wholesome recreational activities. By divine design, fathers are to preside over their families in love and righteousness and are responsible to provide the necessities of life and protection for their families. Mothers are primarily responsible for the nurture of their children. In these sacred responsibilities, fathers and mothers are obligated to help one another as equal partners. Disability, death, or other circumstances may necessitate individual adaptation. Extended families should lend support when needed.[1]

Those are things people must do for us to have a renaissance of happy marriages and productive families. Such a renaissance will require people to try for the ideal – and to keep trying even when the happy result is slow to come and when loud voices mock the effort.

We can and must stand up and defend the institution of marriage between a man and a woman. Professor Lynn Wardle has said: "The task we face is not for summer soldiers or weekend warriors who are willing to work for a season and then quit."[2] A past president of our church, Gordon B. Hinckley, offered similar counsel, as well as encouragement, saying, "We cannot effect a turnaround in a day or a month or a year. But with enough effort, we can begin a turnaround within a generation, and accomplish wonders within two generations."[3]

Today more than a million members of our church in the United States gather their families every day for prayer. Forty-one thousand individual families in Mexico read scriptures together one to three times a week. Seventy thousand individual families in Brazil gather two or three times a month for an evening of prayer, worship, and scripture reading.[4]

Those are small numbers when you think of the billions of parents and families that Heavenly Father watches down upon in this world. But if that family bonding passes through just a few generations, happiness and peace will grow exponentially among the worldwide family of God.

As we work to build and encourage faithful, loving marriages in which men and women become as one and nurture their families, the Lord will multiply our efforts. As we join together in this work, I promise progress toward that happy result. In the name of Jesus Christ, whom I serve and whose witness I am, Amen.

1. "The Family: A Proclamation to the World," *Ensign,* November 2010, 129.
2. Lynn D. Wardle, "The Attack on Marriage as the Union of a Man and a Woman," *North Dakota Law Review,* vol. 83:1387.
3. Gordon B. Hinckley, *Standing for Something* (New York: Times Books, 2000), 170.
4. LDS Church Research Information Division, Member Trends Surveys, 2005–2013; LDS Publishing Services; Richard J. McClendon and Bruce A. Chadwick, "Latter-day Saint Families at the Dawn of the Twenty-First Century," in Craig H. Hart, et al., eds., *Helping and Healing our Families* (Salt Lake City: Deseret Books, 2005).

"We are not created as 'spouse A' and 'spouse B,' but as man and as woman, and in marriage as husband and as wife, in parenting as mother and as father. Masculinity and femininity are not aspects of the fallen order to be overcome, but are instead part of what God declared from the beginning to be 'very good.'"

RUSSELL D. MOORE

16

RUSSELL D. MOORE

Man, Woman, and the Mystery of Christ

A Baptist Perspective

POET WENDELL BERRY responded to the technological utopianism of naturalistic scientism with an observation that I believe frames the entire discussion of what it means to affirm the complementarity of man and woman in marriage. His observation was that any civilization must decide whether it will see persons as machines or as persons. If we are creatures, he argued, then we have meaning and purpose and dignity, but with all of that we have limits. If we see ourselves as machines, then we will believe the Faustian myth of our own limitless power and our ability to reshape even what it means to be human.

This is, it seems to me, the question at the heart of the controversies every culture faces about the meaning of marriage and of sexuality. Are we created, as both the Hebrew Scriptures and Jesus of Nazareth put it, "male and female" from the beginning, or are these categories arbitrary and self-willed? Do our bodies, and our sexes, and our generational connectedness represent something of who we are designed to be, and thus place on us both limits on our ability to recreate ourselves and responsibilities for those who will come after us?

Those of us at this gathering have many differences. We come from different countries, sometimes with tensions between those countries. We hold to different religions, sometimes with great divergences on what we believe about God and about the meaning of life.

But all of us in this room share at least one thing in common. We did not spring into existence out of nothing, but each one of us can trace his or her origins back to a man and a woman, a mother and a father. We recognize that marriage and family are matters of public importance, not just of our various theological and distinctive ecclesial communities. Since marriage is embedded in the created order and is the means of human flourishing, it is not just the arena of individual human desires and appetites. We recognize that marriage, and the sexual difference on which it is built, is grounded in a natural order bearing rights and responsibilities that was not

---

✦ REV. DR. RUSSELL D. MOORE *is president of the Southern Baptist Ethics & Religious Liberty Commission, the Southern Baptist Convention's official entity assigned to address social, moral, and ethical concerns. He speaks frequently on issues of theology, culture, and public policy, and is often quoted or published by the nation's leading news media. He blogs regularly at "Moore to the Point" and is the author or editor of five books and a regular columnist for* Baptist Press. *An ordained minister, Moore has served as pastor for several Southern Baptist churches and as chairman and four-time member of the SBC Resolutions Committee.*

crafted by any human state, and cannot thus be redefined by any human state. It is no accident that questions of marriage and family bring such heated debate, since our consciences, and our very being, testify that these matters are of critical importance for how we shall live.

The purpose of the cosmos

As an evangelical Christian, I come to this discussion with concerns about the common good and human flourishing, but beyond these merely natural goods I have an even deeper concern for what I believe to be the purpose of the entire cosmos: the gospel of Jesus Christ. All of us must stand together on conserving the truth of marriage as a complementary union of man and woman. But I would add that, with that, there is a distinctively Christian urgency for why the Christian churches must bear witness to these things.

The Apostle Paul wrote to the church at Ephesus that the alpha and omega of the universe is personal, that the pattern and goal of the universe is summed up in what he called "the mystery of Christ" (Eph. 1:10). One key aspect of this unveiled mystery is that the family structure is not an arbitrary expression of nature or of the will of God. Marriage and family are instead archetypes, icons of God's purpose for the universe. When the apostle appealed to the Genesis 2 account of the creation order, explaining why a man leaves his father and mother to cleave to his wife, and that they become one flesh (Eph. 5:31), he wrote of something that every human being can see, even without divine revelation. After all, human cultures have died out for a variety of reasons, but no human culture has died out because the people therein forgot to have sexual intercourse. The drive toward marital unity is powerful, so powerful that it can feel as wild as fire. In Paul's Christian theology, this universal truth is because the one-flesh union points beyond itself to the union of Christ and his Church.

In our perspective, the mystery of the gospel explains to us why it was "not good" for the man to be alone, and why Adam wasn't designed to subdivide like an amoeba. He needed someone like him – the beasts of the field were none of them "fit" for him. And yet he needed someone different from him. Fitted together, man and woman form an organic union, as a head with a body. Humanity, then, in the image of God, is created both male and female, with male and female identities that correspond to one another and fulfill one another. We are not created as "spouse A" and "spouse B," but as man and woman, and in marriage as husband and wife, and in parenting as father and mother. Masculinity and femininity are not aspects of the fallen order to be overcome, but are instead part of what God declared from the beginning to be "very good" (Gen. 1:31).

A man is created to be other-directed, to pour himself out for his family. Headship in God's design is not Pharaoh-like tyranny but Christ-like sacrifice. Jesus said of his Church, in its original twelve foundation stones, that he did not call them servants but friends (John 15:15). The relationship between a husband and wife is not that of a business model or a corporate organizational chart but is instead an organic unity. The more a husband and wife are sanctified together in the Word, the more they – like a nervous system and a body – move and operate together smoothly, effortlessly, holistically. They are one flesh, cooperation through complementarity. And in their lives together, as in the life of Christ and his Church, their love is life-giving, including, when God wills, issuing in a new generation.

A different patriarchy

The current debates over whether marriage is a good, over whether children need mothers and fathers, over whether sexual expression should be bound by the covenantal reality of the male–female one-flesh union, spring from a very different reading of the universe, one that assumes an entirely different understanding of human ecology. Western culture now celebrates casual sexuality, cohabitation, no-fault divorce, family redefinition, and abortion rights as parts of a sexual revolution that tore down old patriarchal systems.

But the sexual revolution is not liberation at all, but simply the imposition of a different sort of patriarchy. The sexual revolution empowers men to pursue a Darwinian fantasy of the predatory alpha-male, rooted in the values of power, prestige, and personal pleasure. Does anyone really believe these things will empower women or children? We see the wreckage of sexuality as self-expression all around us, and we will see more yet. And the stakes are not merely social or cultural but profoundly spiritual.

Every culture has recognized that there is something about sexuality that is more than merely the firing of nerve endings, that there is something mysterious here, the joining of selves. In the evangelical Christian perspective, this is because there is no such thing as a casual sexual encounter at all, when we are speaking in spiritual terms. The Apostle Paul warned that the sexually immoral person sins not just against another but "against his own body" (1 Cor. 6:18). He compared the spiritual union formed between Christ and the believer with the union brought about in the sexual act. Even one who is "joined to a prostitute becomes one body with her," he wrote, citing Genesis.

The sexual act, mysteriously, forms a real and personal union. Immorality is not merely "naughtiness," but is a sermon, a sermon preaching a different gospel. This is why attempts to "free" sexuality from marriage as the union of a man and a woman do not lead, ultimately, to the sort of liberation they promise. And therein is our challenge, and our opportunity, for the future.

Encountered "where she is"

In the Gospel of John, Jesus encounters a Samaritan woman by Jacob's Well. The account of their meeting immediately follows the account of his encounter with a religious leader named Nicodemus. The contrasts could not be more striking. Nicodemus was a son of Israel, while the woman was of despised Samaria. Nicodemus was a moral exemplar (or else he wouldn't hold the teaching office); the woman was a moral wreck of indiscretions. Nicodemus came at night; she came at noonday. Jesus encountered both with the gospel, a gospel that is filled, as John put it, with both "truth and grace" (1:17).

The woman wanted to speak of many issues, from biblical arguments about Jacob to theological arguments about temple worship, but Jesus said to her, remarkably, "Go get your husband and come here" (4:16). Both parts of that sentence were necessary. Some would suggest that Jesus should not have addressed the question of her marital status, of her sexual immorality. He should, they would say, have reached her "where she is." But Jesus recognized that this indeed was "where she is." Without addressing the issue of sin, he could not extend the invitation to mercy. The gospel, he told us, comes to sinners only, not to the righteous.

Both truth and grace

Many would tell us that contemporary people will not hear us if we contradict the assumptions of the sexual revolution. We ought to conceal, or at least avoid mentioning, the specifics of what we believe about the definition of marriage, about the limits of human sexuality, about the created and good nature of gender, and speak instead in more generic spiritual terms.

We have heard this before, and indeed we hear it in every generation. Our ancestors were told that modern people could not accept the miraculous claims of the ancient church creeds, and that if we were to reach them "where they are," we should emphasize the ethical content of the Scriptures – the "golden rule" – and de-emphasize the scandal of such things as virgin births and empty tombs and second comings. The churches that followed that path are now deader than Henry VIII. It turns out that people who don't want Christianity don't want almost-Christianity. More importantly, those churches that altered their message adopted what Presbyterian theologian J. Gresham Machen rightly identified as a different religion.

The stakes are just as high now. To jettison or to minimize the Christian sexual ethic is to abandon the message Jesus handed to us, and we have no authority to do this. Moreover, to do so is to abandon our love for our neighbors. We cannot offer the world the half-gospel of a surgical-strike targeted universalism, which exempts from God's judgment those sins we fear are too fashionable to address.

The union of truth and grace is the same biblical tension from which a thousand heresies have sprung. The gospel tells us that God is both "just and the justifier of the one who has faith in Jesus" (Rom. 3:26). The gospel tells us that, left to ourselves, all of us are cut off from the life of God, that we all fall short of the glory of God. The gospel tells us that our only hope is to be joined to another, to be hidden in the righteousness of Jesus Christ, crucified for sinners and raised by the power of God, received through faith. There are always "almost gospels" that seek to circumvent either God's justice or God's mercy.

On the one side, there's the airy antinomianism of those who would seek good news apart from the law and righteousness of God. But such a gospel, severed from the justice of God, is no gospel at all. Indeed, this view suggests that we can approach God without repentance, that we can approach Jesus as a vehicle to heaven but not as Lord, that we can continue in sin that grace may abound (Rom. 6:1). The biblical response couldn't be much stronger: "God forbid!"

On the other side, there is the equally perilous temptation to emphasize the righteousness of God without the invitation to mercy. The Christian gospel tells us that there is life offered to any repentant sinner, and with that life there is a household of belonging, with brothers and sisters, and a place at the table of a joyous wedding feast.

That's why Jesus said to the woman both "Go get your husband" *and* "come here." So must we.

Water for Samaria

Jesus intentionally went to Samaria. His disciples James and John wanted, elsewhere in the Gospel of John, to vaporize the villages there with fire from heaven. But Jesus spoke of water, of living water that could quench thirst forever. Thirst is a type of desperation, the sort of language the Psalmist uses to express the longing for God, as for water in a desert land. We live in a culture obsessed with sex, sex abstracted from covenant, from fidelity, from transcendent moral norms, but beyond this obsession there seems to be a cry for something more.

In the search for sexual excitement, men and women are not really looking for biochemical sensations or the responses of nerve endings. They are searching desperately not merely for sex, but for that to which sex points – for something they know exists but just cannot identify. They are thirsting. As novelist Frederick Buechner put it, "Lust is the craving for salt of someone who is dying of thirst."

The sexual revolution cannot keep its promises. People are looking for a cosmic mystery, for a love that is stronger than death. They cannot articulate it, and perhaps would be horrified to know it, but they are looking for God. The sexual revolution leads to the burned-over boredom of sex shorn of mystery, of relationship shorn of covenant. The question for us, as we pass through the Samaria of the sexual revolution, is whether we have water for Samaria, or if we only have fire. In the wake of the disappointment sexual libertarianism brings, there must be a new word about more permanent things, such as the joy of marriage as a permanent, conjugal, one-flesh reality between a man and a woman. We must keep lit the way to the old paths.

Common grace and gospel mystery

This means that we must both articulate and embody a vision for marriage. We cannot capitulate on these issues. To dispense with marriage is to dispense with a mystery that points to the gospel itself. But we must also create cultures where manhood is defined, not by cultural stereotypes, but by an other-directed, self-sacrificial leadership on behalf of one's family and one's community. We must create cultures where women are valued not for their sexual availability and attractiveness to men but for the sort of fidelity and courage that the Apostle Peter wrote of as that of a "daughter of Sarah" (1 Pet. 3:6). We must work for the common good, in contrast to the sexually libertarian carnivals around us, to speak of the meaning of men and women, of mothers and fathers, of sex and life. We must stand against the will-to-power that reduces children to commodities to be manufactured and as nuisances to be destroyed.

And, as we do so, we should speak publicly of what's at stake. Our neighbors of no religion and of different religions do not recognize a call to gospel mystery. Marriage is a common grace, and we should speak, on their own terms, of why jettisoning normative marriage and family is harmful.

But as a Christian, I am compelled to speak also of the conviction of the Church that what is disrupted when we move beyond the creation design of marriage and family is not just human flourishing but also the picture of the very mystery that defines the existence of the people of God – the gospel of Jesus Christ. With this conviction, we stand and speak not with clenched fists or with wringing hands, but with the open hearts of those who have a message and a mission.

And as we do so, we will remind the world that we are not mere machines of flesh, but rather, we are creatures, accountable to nature and to nature's God. We must do so with the confidence of those who know that on the other side of our culture wars, there's a sexual counter-revolution waiting to be born – again.

Other titles on marriage and family from Plough

Sex, God, and Marriage
Johann Christoph Arnold
Also available in Spanish as *Dios, sexo, y matrimonio*

Why Children Matter
Johann Christoph Arnold
Also available in Spanish as *Porque importan los niños*

Why Forgive?
Johann Christoph Arnold
Also available in Spanish as *Setente veces sieta*

Their Name Is Today
Johann Christoph Arnold
Also available in Spanish as *Su nombre es hoy*

Plough Publishing House
www.plough.com
1-800-521-8011 ◆ 845-572-3455
PO BOX 398 ◆ Walden, NY 12586 ◆ USA
Brightling Rd ◆ Robertsbridge ◆ East Sussex TN32 5DR ◆ UK
4188 Gwydir Highway ◆ Elsmore, NSW 2360 ◆ Australia

HUMANUM

For video of these and other talks, information about events, and short films that highlight the beauty of marriage, visit *humanum.it.*